Coast to Coast in PUNCH NEEDLE

The 50 States, State Flowers, Birds & Trees

Kathi
Xmas 2009

Landauer Books

Coast to Coast in PUNCH NEEDLE
The 50 States, State Flowers, Birds & Trees

This book was designed, produced, and published by Landauer Books
A division of Landauer Corporation
3100 101st Street, Urbandale, IA 50322
www.landauercorp.com   800/557-2144

President/Publisher: Jeramy Lanigan Landauer
Director of Operations: Kitty Jacobson
Managing Editor: Jeri Simon
Art Director: Laurel Albright
Project Editor: Sally Van Nuys
Technical Illustrator: Linda Bender
Illustrator: Thomas Rosborough
Photographer: Craig Anderson Photography

ISBN 10:   0-9793711-4-7
ISBN 13: 978-0-9793711-4-1

Library of Congress Control Number: 2008920302

This book printed on acid-free paper.
Printed in U.S.A.

10-9-8-7-6-5-4-3-2-1

CONTENTS

Special thanks to Ohio artist Sally Van Nuys for designing
and creating the state punch needle projects in this book.
In 2002, she began rug hooking in the primitive style, using wool
strips; punch needle soon followed. She is also a regular
contributor to Create & Decorate magazine. Visit Sally's online
shop at www.amherst-antiques-folkart.com to view her work.

3

BASICS

GETTING STARTED

Learn everything you need to begin your punch needle journey in the Getting Started section. Next choose your destination state and embark on your adventure.

The fabric

The standard fabric used for punch needle embroidery is a medium-weight blend called weaver's cloth. It is a durable and washable fabric in a 50 percent cotton, 50 percent polyester blend. The blend produces a tight, firm weave that holds its shape well—a necessity for successful punch needle.

Weaver's cloth comes in white, natural, and khaki; it can have a lightly flecked appearance that makes it popular for use in country-style home furnishings. It is sold by the piece or by the yard.

The floss

Cotton embroidery floss is inexpensive, easy to use, washable and available in a myriad of colors, making it ideal for punch needle embroidery. Embroidery floss is customarily packaged as a skein consisting of several-yards length of six-stranded thread bundled in a paper wrapper. The six-stranded thread can be easily separated and recombined in the number of strands and colors the punch needle project requires. Most punch needle uses two or three strands of floss in a medium-sized needle. However, you can punch fine details with just one strand, using a smaller needle, or larger areas in six strands, using a larger needle. The projects in this book are based primarily on two-strand punching, with a few optional uses of just one strand.

Floss comes in hundreds of colors and shades, some vat-dyed in solid colors and some hand-dyed in color-on-color. DMC embroidery floss (shown below) is an example of vat-dyed floss. Its 8.7-yard skeins are available in hundreds of solid colors and in metallic finishes. The floss is 100 percent cotton and is both washable and colorfast. Anchor Thread also makes this kind of floss. Both manufacturers sell their floss primarily by color number.

Another kind of floss is hand-dyed in a technique called overdyeing. Like vat-dyed floss, overdyed floss is 100 percent cotton; however the dyes are not colorfast and therefore not suited for use on garments or home furnishings that will need to be washed from time to time. Experienced punch needle specialists use overdyed floss for many special effects, including an antique appearance. If you choose to use overdyed floss, buy enough from the same dye lot to finish your project. Weeks Dye Works produces hand-dyed, overdyed floss in dozens of colors, with 5 yards of six-strand floss in each skein. Sampler Threads™ from The Gentle Art is another floss that is hand-dyed and overdyed to give floss an antique look; it is usually cut in one-yard lengths.

In the state projects featured in this book, yardage amounts and color numbers are given for using two strands of colorfast 100 percent cotton embroidery floss from DMC. The color numbers are accompanied by an unofficial description of DMC colors often used in color charts.

The hoop

Punch needle embroidery works best with a hoop or frame that is designed to allow you to stretch the weaver's cloth to the tightness that punch needle work requires—drum-tight.

A 10-inch hoop was used for the state projects. Be certain to use a hoop with an opening greater than 8 x 8-inches for these projects.

Susan Bates® hoops are designed especially for punch needle use. These hoops come in several sizes, in round and oval shapes, and with a plain finish or in bright colors. The feature that makes Susan Bates hoops so well suited for punch needle work is their "Super-Grip Lip," an extra edge that holds the fabric extra tight, as is required for punch needle.

Similarly, another brand, the "No-Slip Hoop", has a tongue and groove feature around the perimeter of the hoop. Both styles are equipped with thumbscrews for tightening.

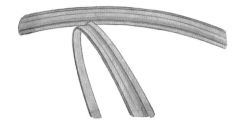

The needle & threader

The traditional Russian punch needle is a slender, hollow shaft. One side of the sharp pointed end is beveled; that is where the eye of the needle is. The thread runs through the length of the needle. These Russian Igolochkoy™ needles come in sets of three sizes, for use with one strand, three strands, or all six strands of embroidery floss.

shown actual size

CTR Needleworks makes the same three needle sizes (each sold separately) of the traditional punch needle, but with several features that make the needle easier to use. It is a little larger and thicker, so it is easier on the hands. Its punching tip has a little silver insert to make the beveled side easier to keep track of, helping you keep the needle in the correct position.

shown actual size

An essential tool required for use with any punch needle is a needle threader, which is made of very thin, stiff wires. The threader is inserted into the needle, the floss is inserted into the threader, and the threader then pulls the thread back through the needle. Threaders ordinarily come with the purchase of the needles, but they can be ordered separately.

The scissors

A pair of small, sharp-pointed and curved-blade embroidery scissors is a necessity for snipping stray floss ends without accidentally snipping off loops. Embroidery scissors come in several sizes and in a variety of designs, shapes, finishes, and of course, prices. There are specialized models for just the left hand or just the right hand, and there are models that can be used in either hand.

The important thing to keep in mind is that your scissors have fine, sharp points and slim, curved blades. Double-curved scissors are especially helpful; they allow you to reach over the

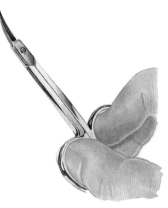

edge of the embroidery hoop while keeping your hand out of the way.

Other helps

There are many needle cases, floss organizers, and storage boxes made specifically for needlework use. Minimally, it is a good idea to have a transparent plastic lidded box that is large enough to hold your equipment and project. Place a magnetic strip into it to keep pins and threaders in place.

A wide array of frames and boxes are available for displaying finished punch needle. Many of the state design motifs can be adapted into projects with a contemporary look and appeal.

Transferring the pattern

Use a transferring pencil, a black scrapbooking pen, a blue sewing pen, or some other fine-tipped, non-bleeding instrument to transfer the pattern to the fabric. Permanent pens and graphite pencils are not recommended because they do not permit

making minor adjustments as you punch; the lines would still show.

To transfer the pattern to the fabric, first use a copier to make a copy of each of the full-size patterns that you plan to use. The state patterns have already been reversed left to right and are ready to use.

If you have access to a light table, lay the paper pattern on the light table, lay the cloth over it, and carefully trace the pattern. You will not punch the lines of the box that appears around the pattern, but use the box to help you line up the design on the straight grain of the fabric.

If you do not have access to a light table, tape the paper pattern to a window that has good light coming through it, tape the cloth over the paper, and trace the pattern.

Loading the hoop

The hoop has two parts; the inner one has an extra lip on its edge, and outer one has the thumbscrew. Lay the inner hoop on the table, lip side up, and lay the fabric over it with the design facing up and centered in the hoop. Loosen the screw on the outer hoop. Lay the outer hoop over the inner hoop and fabric, making sure it pops down over the fabric. The extra lip locks the fabric so you can stretch it.

Begin to secure the fabric, tightening the thumbscrew. Pull the fabric down evenly all around, and tighten the hoop some more. Continue to work around the hoop, using your hand and your fingers to pull down firmly and evenly on the fabric, periodically tightening the hoop some more.

When the fabric is stretched tightly enough, it should sound a little like a snare drum when you tap it. Using a plastic jar gripper will help you tighten the thumbscrew. The rule is, "When you think it is tight, tighten it some more!" The hoop might become slightly distorted.

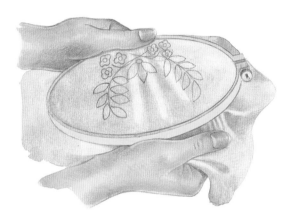

Threading the needle

Hold the wire needle-threader between the thumb and middle finger of your right hand. Holding the needle in your left hand, insert the twisted end of the wire needle-threader through the tip of the needle and out the end of the handle.

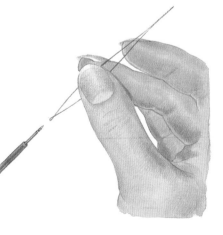

Cut a length of the floss you intend to use first, at least a yard. Carefully separate out two strands (unless otherwise noted). Place several inches of the floss into the opening of the threader.

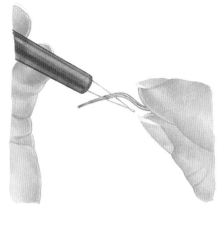

Pull the threader back through the tip of the needle, bringing the two strands of floss along with it until the floss extends several inches beyond the tip of the needle.

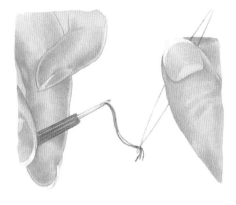

With the floss still in the loop of the threader, insert the other end of the threader into the eye of the needle. Use the threader to pull the floss through the eye of the needle, from the bevel side. Carefully remove the floss from the threader, and put the threader in a secure place (threaders are almost impossible to see if they fall to the floor).

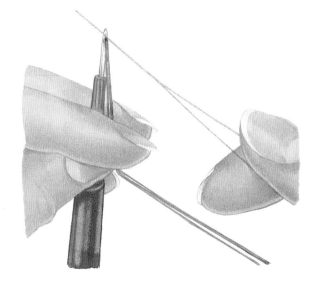

Punching the design

Check the thread to make sure there is nothing to restrict its flow through the needle as you punch. A knot or tangle in the thread can be impossible to remove from the needle casing.

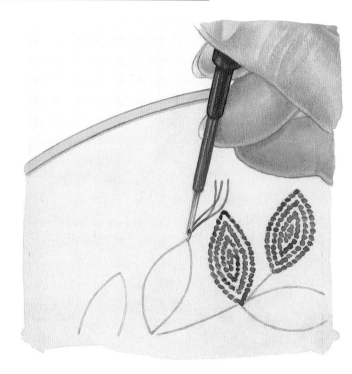

Set your needle for the gauge (depth of loop) you want. Place the needle where you want to start punching. Hold the needle almost perpendicular to the fabric, with the beveled side facing toward where you will punch. If you are right-handed, you will punch from right to left; if you are left-handed, you will punch from left to right.

Firmly push the needle all the way down until it stops. Bring the needle back up, keeping the tip in contact with the fabric to avoid pulling your loop back up. Drag the needle to the next place you want to punch. Leave an opening or two between the stitches; you want a continuous but uncrowded line of loops on the "good" side of the weaver's cloth. After you have several stitches in, leave your needle in the pushed-down position and trim off the "tail" from the first stitch, flush with the fabric. If you want to check your loops for height and spacing, keep the needle down while you turn the the hoop over. When you resume stitching, make sure the bevel faces the next stitch.

Continue punching in a smooth row, "punch, lift, drag, punch."

If you are punching an object, such as a leaf or petal, punch a row just inside the line to outline the object. Then fill it by adding rows of punching, following the object's shape and leaving about a needle's width of space between rows. When you change direction, hold the needle stationary and turn the hoop; this keeps the bevel facing the correct direction.

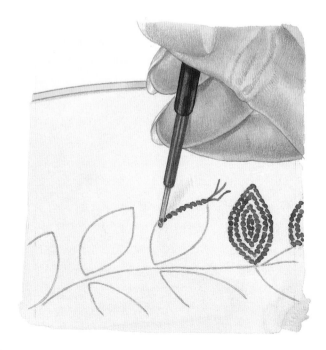

When you finish an area, never drag the thread to the next place you want to punch, even if it is the same color. While the needle is down, turn the hoop over to the front side. Back the needle out just a little (you want it to remain threaded), and use sharp pointed scissors to clip the threads even with the top of your loops so they become part of the pile. Move to the next area you want to punch.

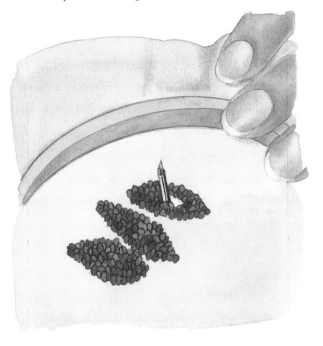

When you need to go to another color, unthread and rethread the needle with the new color. Or, have several needles on hand, each threaded with a different color.

If you make a mistake, pull out the stitches. Use your finger to rub the weave of the cloth back into place, discard the used thread, and punch the stitches again. When you finish, clip any stray ends.

Finishing

Before removing the embroidery from the hoop, check the front of the embroidery for any areas that are not adequately filled. Fill in those areas with the corresponding color, if necessary.

Check the front of the embroidery for any loose tails of thread or long loops. Carefully clip them even with the tops of the other loops. Also, check the back of the embroidery for any long tails and clip them close to the foundation fabric.

Remove the completed design from your hoop.

Stitching your State Punch Needle Design

The patterns in this book are presented in a backward orientation – the state's shape is flipped, and the letters and numbers are backward. You will be punching from the back of the design, therefore, the state and letters and numbers will be in the correct orientation on the front of the design as you stitch.

Follow the Basics instructions to transfer the state patterns onto Weaver's cloth and load it into your hoop. Be sure to trace the pattern straight on the grain of your fabric to ensure that your finished stitching will lay flat and straight when complete.

Use a three-strand punch needle with two strands of embroidery floss, or use a one-strand needle. Stitch just inside all the pattern lines, except where noted, to ensure the proportion of your design stays true. Refer to each state punch needle photo for color reference and placement.

For the majority of the state patterns, set your needle depth gauge on the three-strand needle to 3/8-inch, measuring from the bottom of the gauge to the eye of needle. Some pattern elements will require a shorter loop length or the one-strand needle as indicated in each state's stitching chart.

The state charts list which DMC embroidery floss to use for the design elements, and notes about stitching the pattern. You will need one skein per color unless otherwise noted in the chart. Stitch in the order the chart presents the design elements.

ALABAMA

Entered Union: December 4, 1819
Yellowhammer State
Motto: We Dare Defend Our Rights
Tree: Southern Longleaf Pine
Bird: Yellowhammer
Flower: Camellia

Alabama

Design Element & Order to Stitch	DMC® Embroidery Floss	Notes for Stitching
1. Date	500 Green, dark	Adjust depth gauge to 3/16-inch loop length in one-strand needle. Stitch the date on the pattern lines using one strand of thread. Fill.
2. State Silhouette	915 Fuchsia, dark 917 Fuchsia, medium	Outline state with darker color. Fill with several rows of alternating medium and dark shades.
3. Camellia (leaves/stems)	500 Green, dark (veins/stems) 3345 Green, medium (leaves outline) 988 Green, light (leaves fill)	Stitch veins and stems. Outline and fill leaves with two shades of green.
4. Camellia (flower)	948 Pink, light (petals) 48 Pink, variegated (petals) 320 Sage Green (center pod) 728 Yellow (centers)	Stitch light pink areas. Stitch darker areas with variegated pink floss. Add green center pod and yellow centers with one-strand needle and one strand of floss.
5. Southern Longleaf Pine & Pinecone	500 Green, dark (pine needles) 3371 Brown, dark (pinecone outline) 975/105 Brown shades (pinecone) 3371 Brown, dark (branch outline) 975 Sienna Brown (branch fill)	Stitch pine needles using one strand of thread in one-strand needle with loop gauge set to 1/4-inch. Work two rows for each pine needle, stitching right on pattern lines. Using three-strand needle, stitch on pattern lines of pinecone with darkest brown. Fill pinecone with two lighter shades of brown.
6. State Name	500 Green, dark	Use one-strand needle with gauge set to 3/16-inch loop length to outline and fill letters.
7. Yellowhammer	645 Gray, dark (eye, feet and legs) 3045 Buff/310 Black/321 Red/648 Gray (head) 3829 Brown Gold (beak) 648 Gray (spots) 3045 Buff (breast fill) 975/3829 Brown shades (wing and tail)	Fill areas remaining on branch for feet. Stitch head in buff. Add black, red and gray patches (see photo.) Stitch beak. Outline beneath wing and around tail with dark brown, stitching on pattern lines. Stitch 2-3 stitches of gray for each spot on breast and fill with buff. Stitch dark brown tail feather and wing markings. Fill tail with buff. Fill wing with one strand of each brown indicated.

ALASKA

Entered Union: January 3, 1959
The Last Frontier
Motto: North to the Future
Tree: Sitka Spruce
Bird: Willow Ptarmigan
Flower: Forget-Me-Not

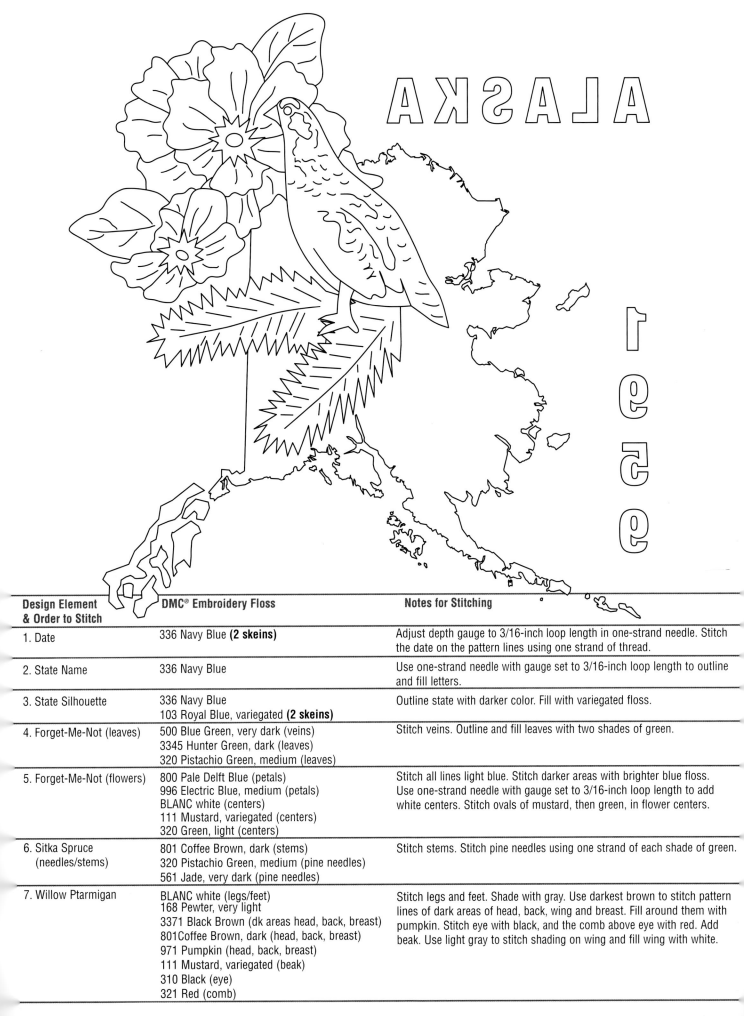

Design Element & Order to Stitch	DMC® Embroidery Floss	Notes for Stitching
1. Date	336 Navy Blue **(2 skeins)**	Adjust depth gauge to 3/16-inch loop length in one-strand needle. Stitch the date on the pattern lines using one strand of thread.
2. State Name	336 Navy Blue	Use one-strand needle with gauge set to 3/16-inch loop length to outline and fill letters.
3. State Silhouette	336 Navy Blue 103 Royal Blue, variegated **(2 skeins)**	Outline state with darker color. Fill with variegated floss.
4. Forget-Me-Not (leaves)	500 Blue Green, very dark (veins) 3345 Hunter Green, dark (leaves) 320 Pistachio Green, medium (leaves)	Stitch veins. Outline and fill leaves with two shades of green.
5. Forget-Me-Not (flowers)	800 Pale Delft Blue (petals) 996 Electric Blue, medium (petals) BLANC white (centers) 111 Mustard, variegated (centers) 320 Green, light (centers)	Stitch all lines light blue. Stitch darker areas with brighter blue floss. Use one-strand needle with gauge set to 3/16-inch loop length to add white centers. Stitch ovals of mustard, then green, in flower centers.
6. Sitka Spruce (needles/stems)	801 Coffee Brown, dark (stems) 320 Pistachio Green, medium (pine needles) 561 Jade, very dark (pine needles)	Stitch stems. Stitch pine needles using one strand of each shade of green.
7. Willow Ptarmigan	BLANC white (legs/feet) 168 Pewter, very light 3371 Black Brown (dk areas head, back, breast) 801 Coffee Brown, dark (head, back, breast) 971 Pumpkin (head, back, breast) 111 Mustard, variegated (beak) 310 Black (eye) 321 Red (comb)	Stitch legs and feet. Shade with gray. Use darkest brown to stitch pattern lines of dark areas of head, back, wing and breast. Fill around them with pumpkin. Stitch eye with black, and the comb above eye with red. Add beak. Use light gray to stitch shading on wing and fill wing with white.

ARIZONA

Entered Union: February 14, 1912
Grand Canyon State
Motto: God Enriches
Tree: Paloverde
Bird: Cactus Wren
Flower: Saguaro Cactus Blossom

1912

ARIZONA

Design Element & Order to Stitch	DMC® Embroidery Floss	Notes for Stitching
1. Date	221 Burgundy	Adjust depth gauge to 3/16-inch loop length in one-strand needle. Stitch the date, using one strand of thread.
2. State Name	221 Burgundy	Use one-strand needle with gauge set to 3/16-inch loop length to outline and fill letters.
3. State Silhouette	107 Pink, variegated (2 skeins) 111 Gold, variegated (2 skeins)	Use one strand of each color in the needle to outline and fill the state shape.
4. Saguaro (cactus)	3011 Olive Green, dark (lines) 469 Olive Green, medium (fill)	Stitch all lines. Fill cactus.
5. Saguaro (flower)	B5200 White (fill) 728 Yellow, dark (lines)	Stitch all lines. Fill flower petals and center.
6. Paloverde	469 Green, medium (stems) 988 Green (leaves)	Stitch stems. Stitch each small leaf.
7. Cactus Wren	3031 Brown, dark (outline) 3371 Brown, darker 610 Brown, medium (wings/back) 612 Brown, light (beak, legs, feet, breast) 310 Black (eye)	Stitch outline. Use darker brown to stitch pattern lines of dark areas of head, back, wing and spots on breast. Stitch eye. Fill wings and back. Add beak, legs and feet. Fill breast.

ARKANSAS

Entered Union: June 15, 1836

The Natural State

Motto: The People Rule

Tree: Shortleaf Pine

Bird: Mockingbird

Flower: Apple Blossom

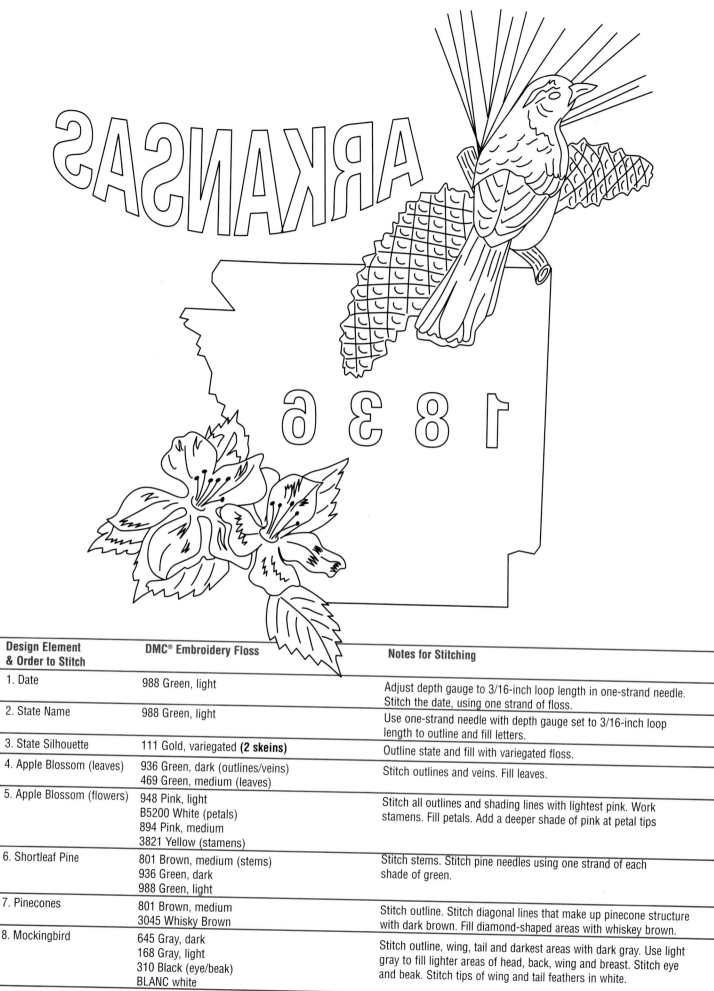

Design Element & Order to Stitch	DMC® Embroidery Floss	Notes for Stitching
1. Date	988 Green, light	Adjust depth gauge to 3/16-inch loop length in one-strand needle. Stitch the date, using one strand of floss.
2. State Name	988 Green, light	Use one-strand needle with depth gauge set to 3/16-inch loop length to outline and fill letters.
3. State Silhouette	111 Gold, variegated (2 skeins)	Outline state and fill with variegated floss.
4. Apple Blossom (leaves)	936 Green, dark (outlines/veins) 469 Green, medium (leaves)	Stitch outlines and veins. Fill leaves.
5. Apple Blossom (flowers)	948 Pink, light B5200 White (petals) 894 Pink, medium 3821 Yellow (stamens)	Stitch all outlines and shading lines with lightest pink. Work stamens. Fill petals. Add a deeper shade of pink at petal tips
6. Shortleaf Pine	801 Brown, medium (stems) 936 Green, dark 988 Green, light	Stitch stems. Stitch pine needles using one strand of each shade of green.
7. Pinecones	801 Brown, medium 3045 Whisky Brown	Stitch outline. Stitch diagonal lines that make up pinecone structure with dark brown. Fill diamond-shaped areas with whiskey brown.
8. Mockingbird	645 Gray, dark 168 Gray, light 310 Black (eye/beak) BLANC white	Stitch outline, wing, tail and darkest areas with dark gray. Use light gray to fill lighter areas of head, back, wing and breast. Stitch eye and beak. Stitch tips of wing and tail feathers in white.

CALIFORNIA

Entered Union: September 9, 1850
Golden State
Motto: Eureka—I Have Found It
Tree: Native Redwood
(Coast Redwood and Giant Sequoia)
Bird: California Quail
Flower: Golden Poppy

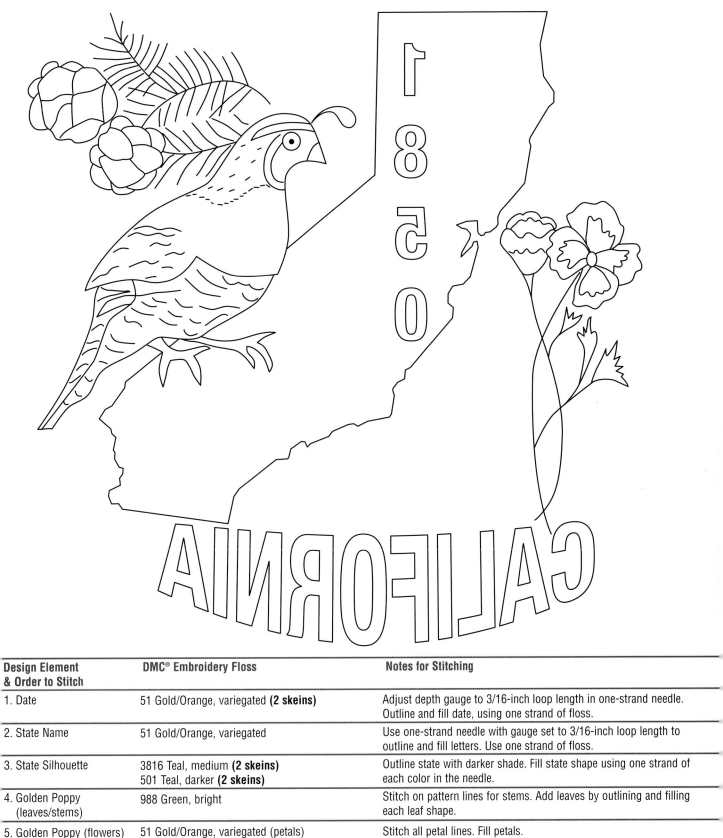

Design Element & Order to Stitch	DMC® Embroidery Floss	Notes for Stitching
1. Date	51 Gold/Orange, variegated **(2 skeins)**	Adjust depth gauge to 3/16-inch loop length in one-strand needle. Outline and fill date, using one strand of floss.
2. State Name	51 Gold/Orange, variegated	Use one-strand needle with gauge set to 3/16-inch loop length to outline and fill letters. Use one strand of floss.
3. State Silhouette	3816 Teal, medium **(2 skeins)** 501 Teal, darker **(2 skeins)**	Outline state with darker shade. Fill state shape using one strand of each color in the needle.
4. Golden Poppy (leaves/stems)	988 Green, bright	Stitch on pattern lines for stems. Add leaves by outlining and filling each leaf shape.
5. Golden Poppy (flowers)	51 Gold/Orange, variegated (petals) 728 Gold (petal lines)	Stitch all petal lines. Fill petals.
6. Giant Redwood (needles, pinecones, stems)	975 Burnt Sienna Brown (stems) 936 Pine Green (pine needles) 3371 Brown, dark (pinecone lines) 105 Brown, variegated (fill)	Stitch stems first using two strands of thread. Stitch pine needles using one strand green thread. Stitch two rows for each pine needle. Stitch all pinecone lines. Fill with variegated brown.
7. California Quail	975 Burnt Sienna Brown (legs/feet) 3371 Brown, dark (head, back, tail) B5200 White (head) 612/610 Tans (body/tail); 612 Tan, light (beak) 310 Black (eye); 645 Gray (head/wing)	Stitch legs and feet. Stitch on the pattern lines of dark areas of head, back, wing and tail. Fill around them with two colors of tan. Stitch eye. Stitch topknot feather with dark brown and gray. Add beak. Use solid gray to stitch lines on back of head and breast/wing. Fill those areas with one strand of gray and one strand of white in the needle to create a mottled, gray fill color.

COLORADO

Entered Union: August 1, 1876
Centennial State
Motto: Nothing Without Providence
Tree: Colorado Blue Spruce
Bird: Lark Bunting
Flower: Rocky Mountain Columbine

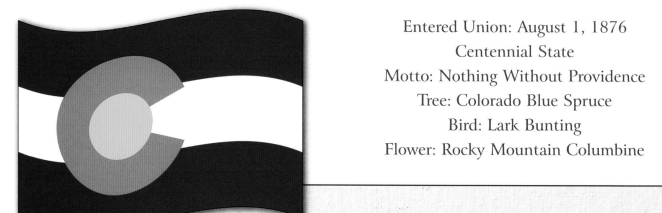

Design Element & Order to Stitch	DMC® Embroidery Floss	Notes for Stitching
1. Date	3857 Rosewood, dark **(2 skeins)**	Adjust depth gauge to 3/16-inch loop length in one-strand needle. Outline and fill date, using one strand of floss.
2. State Name	3857 Rosewood, dark	Use one-strand needle with gauge set to 3/16-inch loop length to outline and fill letters, using one strand of floss.
3. Columbine	3839 Lavender Blue, medium (spurs) B5200 Snow White (large petals) 3821 Straw (center)	Use two strands in the three-strand needle to outline and fill the lavender spur petals and shading on the large petals. Stitch the larger white petals. Add the center to the flower.
4. Blue Spruce	975 Golden Brown, dark (stems) 320 Pistachio Green, medium (pine needles)	Stitch stems using two strands of thread. Stitch each pine needle, keeping stitches close and even. Stitch one row for each pine needle.
5. Lark Bunting	975 Golden Brown, dark (feet) 310 Black (outline, back, head, wing, tail, breast) B5200 White (wing, back, tail) 645 Beaver Gray, very dark (head/breast) 648 Beaver Gray, light (head/breast	Stitch feet. Outline entire bird shape with black, and then stitch black areas of head, back, breast and tail (refer to photo for placement.) Stitch white areas. Add light and dark gray to head and breast.
6. State Silhouette	976 Golden Brown, medium **(2 skeins)**	Outline state shape and fill in around overlapping design elements to fill state shape completely. Take care not to bury the pine needles as you stitch around them.

CONNECTICUT

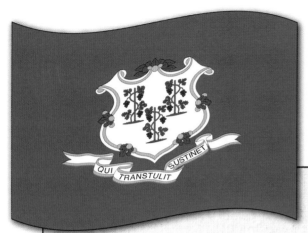

Entered Union: January 9, 1788
Constitution State
Motto: He Who Transplants Still Sustains
Tree: White Oak
Bird: American Robin
Flower: Mountain Laurel

Design Element & Order to Stitch	DMC® Embroidery Floss	Notes for Stitching
1. Date	103 Royal Blue, variegated	Adjust depth gauge to 3/16-inch loop length in one-strand needle. Stitch the date on the pattern lines. Repeat with second row.
2. State Name	103 Royal Blue, variegated	Use one-strand needle with gauge set to 3/16-inch loop length to stitch the name on the pattern lines. Repeat with second row.
3. American Robin	310 Black (head, eye, wing lines) BLANC white (around eye, throat, above legs) 725 Topaz (beak) 3031 Mocha Brown, dark (back, wing, tail areas) 610 Drab Brown, dark (light areas back, wing, tail) 720 Orange Spice, dark (breast) 801 Coffee Brown, dark (legs)	Stitch head and eye. Add beak. Use black and white for small area of throat. Stitch black pattern lines on wing and fill darkest brown areas on back, wing and tail. Add lighter brown areas on back, wing and tail (refer to photo). Outline and fill breast. Add small area of white above the legs. Stitch legs.
4. White Oak (leaves/acorns)	94 Khaki Green, variegated (veins) 469 Avocado Green (fill) 612 Drab Brown, light (acorns) 610 Drab Brown, dark (acorns)	Stitch leaf veins and fill leaves. Use two shades of brown for acorns.
5. Mountain Laurel (buds)	3823 Ultra Pale Yellow (buds) 469 Avocado Green	Stitch buds. Fill behind them with green to resemble foliage.
6. Mountain Laurel (flowers)	894 Carnation, very light (outlines) 948 Peach, very light (fill) 725 Topaz (centers)	Stitch outlines. Fill with lighter shade. Add centers.
7. State Sillhouette	932 Antique Blue, light (2 skeins)	Outline state and fill.

DELAWARE

DECEMBER 7, 1787

Entered Union: December 7, 1787
The First State
Motto: Liberty and Independence
Tree: American Holly
Bird: Blue Hen Chicken
Flower: Peach Blossom

Design Element & Order to Stitch	DMC® Embroidery Floss	Notes for Stitching
1. Date	976 Golden Brown, medium	Adjust depth gauge to 3/16-inch loop length in one-strand needle. Outline and fill the date.
2. State Name	976 Golden Brown, medium	Use one-strand needle with gauge set to 3/16-inch loop length to outline and fill the state name.
3. Blue Hen	349 Coral, dark (comb, around eye, waddle) 310 Black (eye/accents) 725 Topaz (beak/neck) 168 Silver Gray (legs, breast, neck accent) 931 Antique Blue, medium (breast, wing, tail) 800 Pale Delft Blue (breast/wing) 996 Electric Blue (neck, breast, wing, tail)	Stitch comb, waddle and around eye. Add beak and eye. Refer to photo and use combination of blues and gray to stitch hen. Add accents of black and topaz. Stitch the legs.
4. Holly (tree)	320 Pistachio Green, medium (outline) 733 Olive Green, medium (medium) 500 Blue Green, dark (fill) 975 Golden Brown, dark (stem) 321 Red (berries)	Outline leaves. Stitch leaf veins and fill leaves. Add stem and berries.
5. Peach Blossom (flowers)	107 Carnation, variegated (outlines/fill) 111 Mustard, variegated (centers)	Stitch petal outlines and fill. Add centers.
6. State Sillhouette	371 Mustard (2 skeins)	Outline state and fill.

FLORIDA

Entered Union: March 3, 1845
Sunshine State
Motto: In God We Trust
Tree: Sabal Palmetto
Bird: Mockingbird
Flower: Orange Blossom

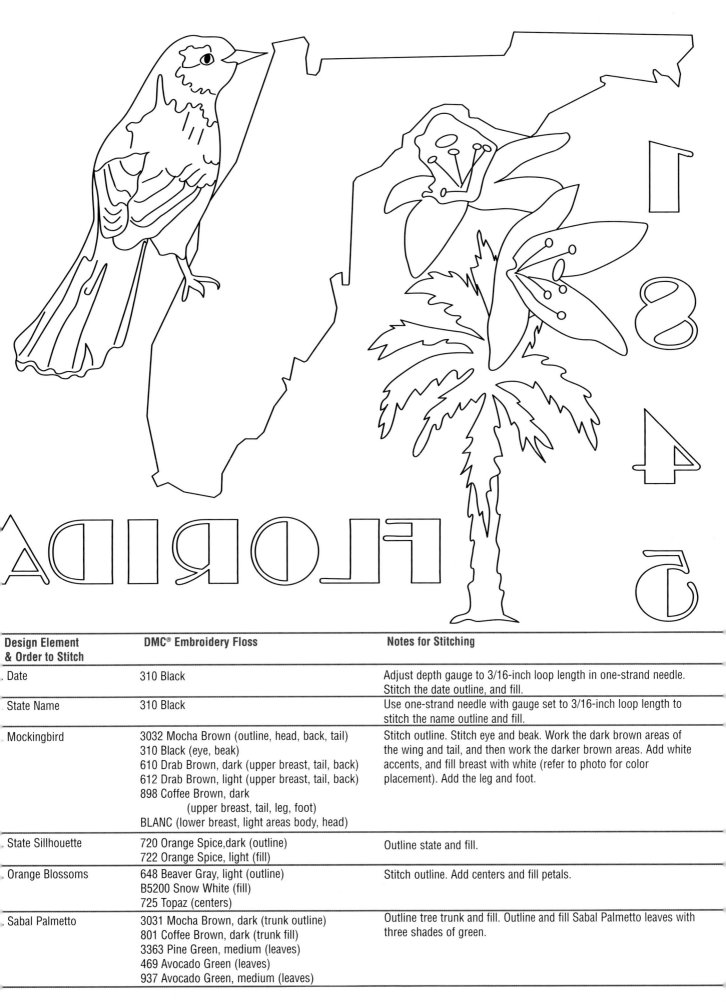

Design Element & Order to Stitch	DMC® Embroidery Floss	Notes for Stitching
Date	310 Black	Adjust depth gauge to 3/16-inch loop length in one-strand needle. Stitch the date outline, and fill.
State Name	310 Black	Use one-strand needle with gauge set to 3/16-inch loop length to stitch the name outline and fill.
Mockingbird	3032 Mocha Brown (outline, head, back, tail) 310 Black (eye, beak) 610 Drab Brown, dark (upper breast, tail, back) 612 Drab Brown, light (upper breast, tail, back) 898 Coffee Brown, dark (upper breast, tail, leg, foot) BLANC (lower breast, light areas body, head)	Stitch outline. Stitch eye and beak. Work the dark brown areas of the wing and tail, and then work the darker brown areas. Add white accents, and fill breast with white (refer to photo for color placement). Add the leg and foot.
State Sillhouette	720 Orange Spice, dark (outline) 722 Orange Spice, light (fill)	Outline state and fill.
Orange Blossoms	648 Beaver Gray, light (outline) B5200 Snow White (fill) 725 Topaz (centers)	Stitch outline. Add centers and fill petals.
Sabal Palmetto	3031 Mocha Brown, dark (trunk outline) 801 Coffee Brown, dark (trunk fill) 3363 Pine Green, medium (leaves) 469 Avocado Green (leaves) 937 Avocado Green, medium (leaves)	Outline tree trunk and fill. Outline and fill Sabal Palmetto leaves with three shades of green.

GEORGIA

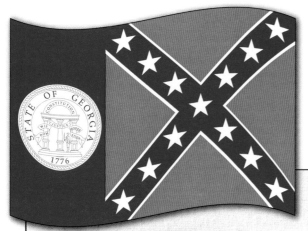

Entered Union: January 2, 1788
Peach State
Motto: Wisdom, Justice, and Moderation
Tree: Live Oak
Bird: Brown Thrasher
Flower: Cherokee Rose

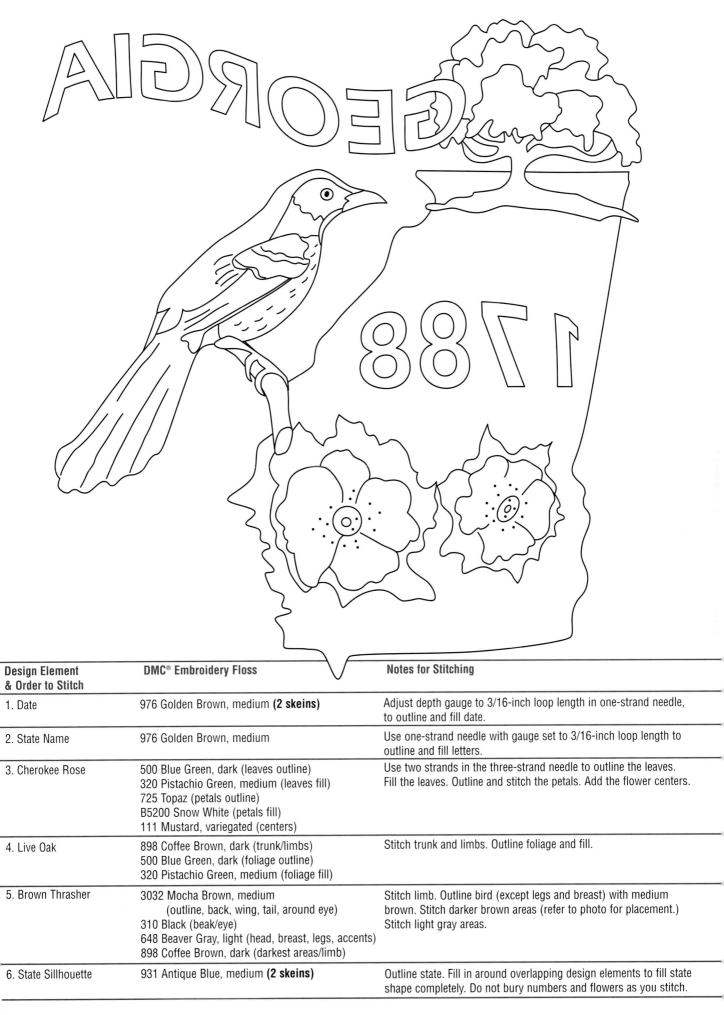

Design Element & Order to Stitch	DMC® Embroidery Floss	Notes for Stitching
1. Date	976 Golden Brown, medium **(2 skeins)**	Adjust depth gauge to 3/16-inch loop length in one-strand needle, to outline and fill date.
2. State Name	976 Golden Brown, medium	Use one-strand needle with gauge set to 3/16-inch loop length to outline and fill letters.
3. Cherokee Rose	500 Blue Green, dark (leaves outline) 320 Pistachio Green, medium (leaves fill) 725 Topaz (petals outline) B5200 Snow White (petals fill) 111 Mustard, variegated (centers)	Use two strands in the three-strand needle to outline the leaves. Fill the leaves. Outline and stitch the petals. Add the flower centers.
4. Live Oak	898 Coffee Brown, dark (trunk/limbs) 500 Blue Green, dark (foliage outline) 320 Pistachio Green, medium (foliage fill)	Stitch trunk and limbs. Outline foliage and fill.
5. Brown Thrasher	3032 Mocha Brown, medium (outline, back, wing, tail, around eye) 310 Black (beak/eye) 648 Beaver Gray, light (head, breast, legs, accents) 898 Coffee Brown, dark (darkest areas/limb)	Stitch limb. Outline bird (except legs and breast) with medium brown. Stitch darker brown areas (refer to photo for placement.) Stitch light gray areas.
6. State Sillhouette	931 Antique Blue, medium **(2 skeins)**	Outline state. Fill in around overlapping design elements to fill state shape completely. Do not bury numbers and flowers as you stitch.

HAWAII

Entered Union: August 21, 1959
Aloha State
Motto: The Life of the Land is
Perpetuated in Righteousness
Tree: Kukui (Candlenut Tree)
Bird: Nene (Hawaiian Goose)
Flower: Pua Aloalo (Yellow Hibiscus)

Design Element & Order to Stitch	DMC® Embroidery Floss	Notes for Stitching
1. State Name	597 Turquoise **(2 skeins)**	Adjust depth gauge to 3/16-inch loop length in one-strand needle, to outline and fill state name.
2. Date	597 Turquoise	Use one-strand needle with gauge set to 3/16-inch loop length to outline and fill date.
3. Kukui (tree)	520 Fern Green, dark (veins/stems) 522 Fern Green, light (leaves) 829 Golden Olive, dark (branch) 642 Beige Gray, dark (candlenut) 3823 Ultra Pale Yellow (flowers)	Stitch veins and stems. Outline and fill leaves. Stitch branch and add candlenut with beige gray. Add ivory flowers with pale yellow.
4. Pua Aloalo (flower)	733 Olive Green, medium (outline) 725 Topaz, medium 834 Golden Olive, light 111 Mustard, variegated	Stitch petal outlines. Fill petals with a mix of yellows with some darker gold shadows. Set gauge to 1/2-inch loop length to add centers.
5. Nene (bird)	310 Black (beak, head/neck, under wing) 612 Drab Brown, light 3031 Mocha Brown, dark 3823 Ultra Pale Yellow	Outline and fill back areas, adding a bit of black on wing to define. Use lightest brown to define eye and beak markings. Outline and fill dark brown areas, adding light brown and pale yellow to define feathers and light areas. Fill light brown areas on neck and beneath tail feathers. See photo for precise color placement.
6. State Sillhouette	597 Turquoise	Outline and fill island silhouettes.

IDAHO

Entered Union: July 3, 1890
Gem State
Motto: It is Perpetual
Tree: Western White Pine
Bird: Mountain Bluebird
Flower: Syringa

Design Element & Order to Stitch	DMC® Embroidery Floss	Notes for Stitching
1. State Name	103 Blue, variegated (2 skeins)	Stitch the state name on the pattern lines and fill.
2. Date	103 Blue, variegated	Stitch the date on the pattern lines and fill.
3. Syringa (foliage)	500 Blue Green, dark (veins/stems, outline) 522 Fern Green (leaves)	Stitch veins and outline leaves. Fill leaves. Stitch stems.
4. Syringa (flowers)	762 Pearl Gray, light (outlines) BLANC white (fill) 111 Mustard, variegated (centers)	Stitch petal and bud outlines, then fill. Use one-strand needle with gauge set to 3/16-inch loop length to add centers.
5. Western White Pine	610 Drab Brown, dark (branches) 500 Blue Green, dark (pine needles) 3364 Pine Green (pine needles) 3031 Mocha Brown, dark (pinecone outline) 642 Beige Gray, dark (pinecone fill) 610 Drab Brown, dark (pinecone fill)	Outline branches and fill. Stitch single rows of dark green and light green to form pine needles. Outline pinecone. Fill pinecone with various shades of brown to add dimension and texture.
6. Mountain Bluebird	931 Antique Blue, medium (wing, head) 597 Turquoise (body) 800 Pale Delft Blue (lower body) 310 Black (beak, eye, feet, wing markings)	Outline and fill black areas. Outline and fill light areas. Stitch beak and feet.
7. State Silhouette	976 Golden Brown, medium (2 skeins)	Outline and fill state silhouette.

ILLINOIS

Entered Union: December 3, 1818
Prairie State
Motto: State Sovereignty—National Union
Tree: White Oak
Bird: Cardinal
Flower: Violet

Design Element & Order to Stitch	DMC® Embroidery Floss	Notes for Stitching
1. State Name	161 Gray Blue **(2 skeins)**	Adjust depth gauge to 3/16-inch loop length in one-strand needle to outline and fill state name.
2. Date	161 Gray Blue	Use one-strand needle with gauge set to 3/16-inch loop length to outline and fill date.
3. White Oak	94 Khaki Green, variegated (veins/stem) 3363 Pine Green, medium (leaf) 520 Fern Green, dark (leaf)	Stitch veins and stem. Outline and fill leaf with dark and medium greens.
4. Native Violet	728 Topaz (center) 162 Ultra Light Blue (around center) 161 Gray Blue (petals) 3364 Pine Green, light (stems/leaves/ground line) 3363 Pine Green, medium (leaves) 520 Fern Green, dark (leaf)	Stitch centers. Add light blue around centers and to define petal edges. Outline and fill petals. Stitch stems and tops of leaves in light green, fill bottoms of leaves with medium green, and tops with dark green. Stitch ground line in light green.
5. Cardinal	310 Black (eye, face, wing, tail) BLANC white (around eye) 321 Red (body) 728 Topaz (beak, legs)	Outline and fill black areas, adding a bit of black on wing to define. Stitch beak and legs. Outline and fill body. See photo for placement.
6. State Sillhouette	783 Topaz, medium **(2 skeins)** 782 Topaz, dark 834 Golden Olive, light	Outline and fill state silhouette with medium topaz. Fill most of state with medium topaz, adding small areas with darker and lighter colors for some interest.

INDIANA

Entered Union: December 11, 1816

Hoosier State

Motto: Crossroads of America

Tree: Tulip Poplar

Bird: Cardinal

Flower: Peony

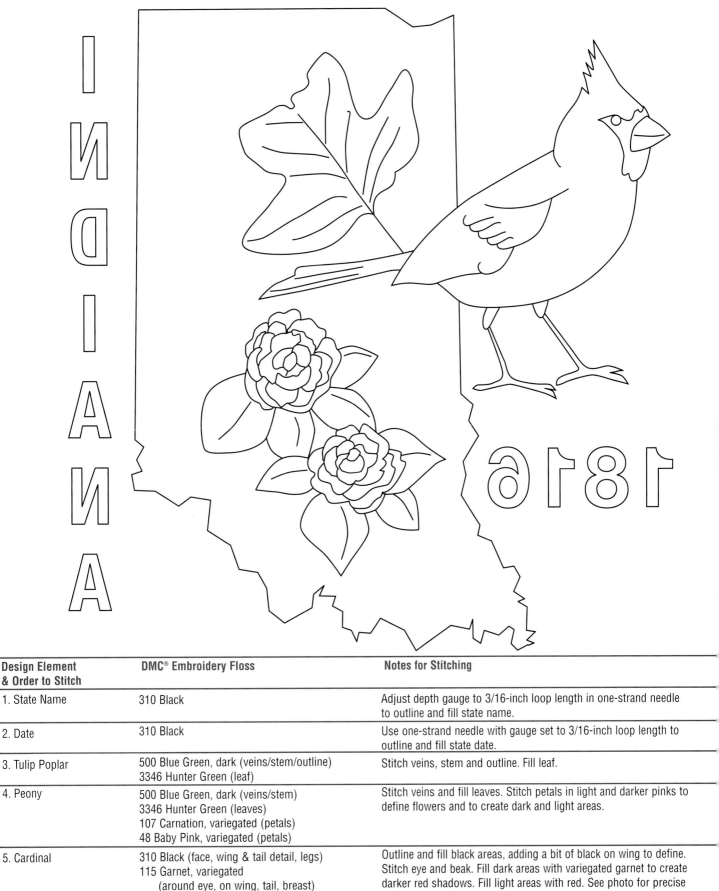

Design Element & Order to Stitch	DMC® Embroidery Floss	Notes for Stitching
1. State Name	310 Black	Adjust depth gauge to 3/16-inch loop length in one-strand needle to outline and fill state name.
2. Date	310 Black	Use one-strand needle with gauge set to 3/16-inch loop length to outline and fill state date.
3. Tulip Poplar	500 Blue Green, dark (veins/stem/outline) 3346 Hunter Green (leaf)	Stitch veins, stem and outline. Fill leaf.
4. Peony	500 Blue Green, dark (veins/stem) 3346 Hunter Green (leaves) 107 Carnation, variegated (petals) 48 Baby Pink, variegated (petals)	Stitch veins and fill leaves. Stitch petals in light and darker pinks to define flowers and to create dark and light areas.
5. Cardinal	310 Black (face, wing & tail detail, legs) 115 Garnet, variegated (around eye, on wing, tail, breast) 321 Red (body) 728 Topaz (beak, legs, eye)	Outline and fill black areas, adding a bit of black on wing to define. Stitch eye and beak. Fill dark areas with variegated garnet to create darker red shadows. Fill light areas with red. See photo for precise color placement.
6. State Sillhouette	3045 Yellow Beige, dark **(3 skeins)** 437 Tan, light 976 Golden Brown, medium	Outline state silhouette with medium value. Fill most of the state with medium value, adding small areas with darker and lighter values for some interest.

IOWA

Entered Union: December 28, 1846
Hawkeye State
Motto: Our Liberties We Prize,
and Our Rights We Will Maintain
Tree: Oak
Bird: Eastern Goldfinch
Flower: Wild Prairie Rose

Design Element & Order to Stitch	DMC® Embroidery Floss	Notes for Stitching
1. State Name	3857 Rosewood, dark **(3 skeins)**	Stitch the state name on the pattern lines and fill.
2. Date	3857 Rosewood, dark 221 Shell Pink, very dark	Outline and fill numbers 8 and 6 with darker color. Outline and fill numbers 1 and 4 with lighter color.
3. Wild Prairie Rose (leaves)	500 Blue Green, dark (outline/fill) 469 Avocado green (veins)	Stitch veins. Outline and fill leaves.
4. Wild Prairie Rose (flowers)	3857 Rosewood, dark (outlines) 107 Carnation, variegated (fill) 894 Carnation, light (fill) 728 Golden Yellow (centers) BLANC white (centers)	Stitch petal outlines. Fill petals with light and medium shades of pink. Use one-strand needle with gauge set to 3/16-inch loop length to add yellow centers. Stitch ovals of white in flower centers.
5. Oak	433 Brown, medium (trunk/limbs) 167 Yellow Beige, dark (highlight trunk/limbs) 500 Blue Green, dark (leaves) 469 Avocado Green (veins)	Outline trunk and limbs, and fill. Highlight up center of trunk and limbs. Stitch veins of leaves and fill.
6. Eastern Goldfinch	310 Black (wing, head, tail) 728 Golden Yellow (body) 111 Mustard, variegated (beak, feet) BLANC white (markings on wing) 167 Yellow Beige (outline & highlight limb) 433 Brown, medium (fill limb)	Outline and fill black areas, adding white on wing. Outline and fill body. Stitch beak and feet. Outline, highlight, and fill limb.
7. State Sillhouette	3857 Rosewood, dark	Outline and fill state silhouette. Take care not to snag bird or flowers as you fill around them.

KANSAS

Entered Union: January 29, 1861
Sunflower State
Motto: To the Stars Through Difficulties
Tree: Cottonwood
Bird: Western Meadowlark
Flower: Wild Native Sunflower

Design Element & Order to Stitch	DMC® Embroidery Floss	Notes for Stitching
1. Date	608 Bright Orange	Adjust depth gauge to 3/16-inch loop length in one-strand needle. Stitch the date just inside the pattern lines, using one strand of thread. Fill the numbers.
2. State Name	500 Blue Green, dark	Use one-strand needle with gauge set to 3/16-inch loop length to outline and fill letters.
3. Sunflower (leaves/stems)	500 Blue Green, dark (veins/fill/outline) 520 Fern Green, dark (stem)	Stitch veins. Outline and fill leaves. Outline and fill stem.
4. Sunflower	3371 Black Brown (center/swirls) 111 Mustard, variegated 300 Mahogany, dark 728 Golden Yellow (petal fill)	Work center first, then add swirls around it. Fill between swirls with mahogany and variegated mustard. Use variegated mustard to separate outer petals by outlining some of them. Fill petals.
5. Cottonwood	433 Brown, medium 3371 Black Brown	Beginning with smaller twigs at branch ends, stitch right on pattern lines with one row of medium brown. Outline and fill branches with medium brown. Add dark brown shadows. Using medium brown outline and fill trunk, adding dark brown shading along one side.
6. Western Meadowlark	3371 Black Brown 3821 Straw (head/breast) ECRU 976 Golden Brown, medium (legs)	Use black brown to outline top of bird and under wing. Add eye with several loops of black brown. Stitch dark brown spots on back and lines between wing and breast. Outline and fill head and breast. Add yellow beneath the tail. Fill remaining areas with off-white. Outline and fill legs.
7. Rock Perch	433 Brown, medium 3371 Black Brown	With one strand of each color brown in the needle, outline and fill the rock perch.
8. State Silhouette	971 Pumpkin 608 Bright Orange (1 skein each)	Outline and fill state. Take care not to snag loops of other elements.

KENTUCKY

Entered Union: June 1, 1792
Bluegrass State
Motto: United We Stand, Divided We Fall
Tree: Tulip Poplar
Bird: Cardinal
Flower: Goldenrod

Design Element & Order to Stitch	DMC® Embroidery Floss	Notes for Stitching
1. Date	115 Garnet, variegated	Adjust depth gauge to 3/16-inch loop length in one-strand needle. stitch the date just inside the pattern lines. Fill the numbers with one strand of thread.
2. State Name	115 Garnet, variegated	Use one-strand needle with gauge set to 3/16-inch loop length to outline and fill letters.
3. State Sillhouette	502 Blue Green (2 skeins)	Outline state and fill.
4. Goldenrod (leaves/stems)	94 Khaki Green, varigated	Stitch veins. Outline and fill leaves.
5. Goldenrod (petals)	90 Yellow, variegated	Outline and fill goldenrod flowers. The variegated thread will create shadows and highlights as you stitch.
6. Tulip Poplar (leaf)	936 Avocado Green, dark (outline, veins, stem) 469 Avocado (fill)	Outline leaf. Stitch veins and stem. Fill leaf.
7. Cardinal	321 Red (main body) 976 Golden Brown, medium (beak, feet) 111 Mustard, variegated (beak) 310 Black (head, eye, shadows) 3011 Khaki Green, dark (stick)	Stitch shadows along wings and tail with black. Outline and fill black areas on head. Add eye pupil. Create stick with three rows of khaki green. Add feet around stick. Stitch bottom of beak with golden brown, and stitch top of beak with mustard. Stitch around eye with mustard. Fill in body of cardinal.

LOUISIANA

UNION, JUSTICE & CONFIDENCE

Entered Union: April 30, 1812
Pelican State
Motto: Union, Justice, and Confidence
Tree: Bald Cypress
Bird: Brown Pelican
Flower: Magnolia Blossom

Design Element & Order to Stitch	DMC® Embroidery Floss	Notes for Stitching
1. Date	597 Turquoise	Adjust depth gauge to 3/16-inch loop length in one-strand needle. Stitch date right on the pattern lines and fill the numbers.
2. State Name	597 Turquoise	Use one-strand needle with gauge set to 3/16-inch loop length to outline and fill letters.
3. Magnolia (leaves)	435 Brown, light (veins) 3346 Hunter Green (fill)	Stitch veins and fill leaves.
4. Magnolia (flower)	3023 Brown Gray, light (outline) 435 Brown, light (center) WHITE (fill)	Outline petals. Add center and fill petals with white.
5. Bald Cypress (tree)	830 Golden Olive, dark (branch, pinecone outlines) 642 Beige Gray, dark (pinecone fill) 520 Fern Green (pine needles)	Stitch branch. Stitch pinecone outline and division lines. Fill diamonds of pinecone. Using fern green stitch one row for each pine needle.
6. Brown Pelican	3371 Black Brown 　(neck, beak outline, feet, eye, shadows) 111 Mustard, variegated (head, throat) 3023 Brown Gray, light (beak, body) ECRU (head, body)	Outline beak and fill dark area of neck. Stitch and fill remaining dark areas on body and add eye. Stitch and fill gold areas on head and throat. Fill beak with brown gray, and then fill gray areas on body. Fill remaining areas on body with ecru.
7. Tree Stump	300 Mahogany, dark (side) 3371 Black Brown (lines) 642 Beige Gray, dark (highlights) 435 Brown, light (sides/top)	Outline top of stump with black brown. Add crack lines. Outline bottom section with beige gray and fill with brown and mahogany (see photo for placement reference.)
8. State Silhouette	350 Coral Red, medium (**2 skeins**)	Outline state and fill. Take care not to snag the loops of the bird.

MAINE

Entered Union: March 15, 1820
Pine Tree State
Motto: I Direct
Tree: Eastern White Pine
Bird: Black-capped Chickadee
Flower: White Pine Cone and Tassel

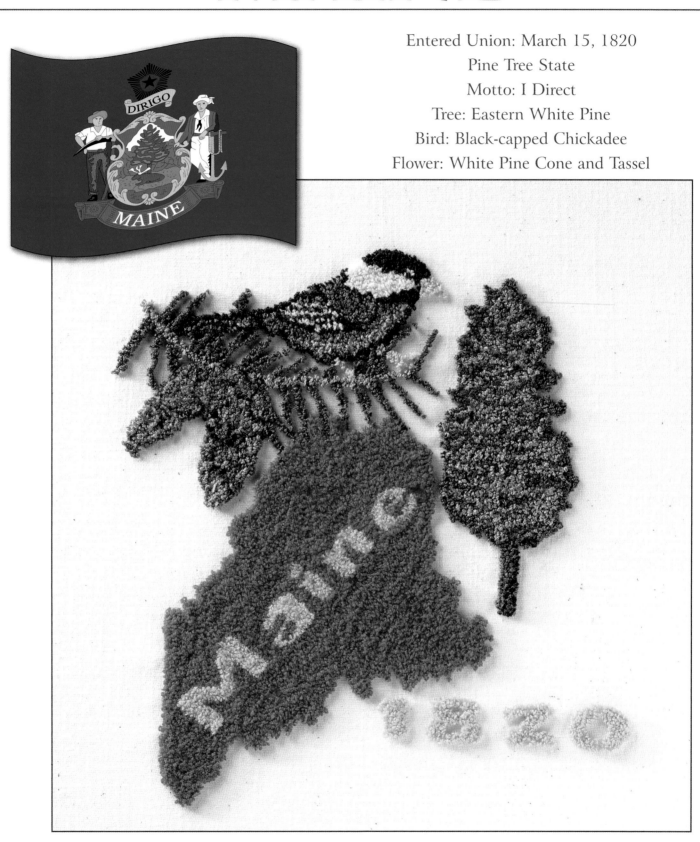

48

Design Element & Order to Stitch	DMC® Embroidery Floss	Notes for Stitching
1. Date	728 Topaz	Adjust depth gauge to 3/16-inch loop length in one-strand needle to outline and fill date.
2. State Name	728 Topaz	Use one-strand needle with gauge set to 3/16-inch loop length to outline and fill letters.
3. State Sillhouette	817 Coral Red, dark (2 skeins)	Outline state and fill, leaving space for overlap of pine needles.
4. Pinecone	830 Golden Olive, dark (outlines) 642 Beige Gray, dark (fill) 3371 Black Brown (shading)	Stitch outlines and division lines of pinecone. Fill diamonds of pinecone with gray and black brown.
5. Pine Tassel	302 Gray (branch) 520 Fern Green, dark (pine needles)	Stitch branch. Stitch two rows of green for each pine needle.
6. Eastern White Pine (tree)	830 Golden Olive, dark (trunk) 3371 Black Brown (shading trunk) 520 Fern Green, dark (outline/shading) 522 Fern Green (fill)	Stitch trunk. Outline pine tree. Stitch pine tree foliage using two colors of green to create shading.
7. Black-capped Chickadee	ECRU (head/wing) 610 Drab Brown, dark (back, wing, tail, body) 3371 Black Brown (head, eye, markings, outline) 728 Topaz (beak/legs)	Stitch eye, and then stitch several loops of ecru around it. Stitch outline and fill area on neck with ecru. Use black brown to stitch outlines of dark areas of head, back, wing and breast. Outline entire body. Fill dark areas on head and throat. Add beak and legs. Use brown to stitch lines on wing and fill with ecru. Fill upper body. With one strand of brown and one strand of ecru in needle, stitch breast.

MARYLAND

Entered Union: April 28, 1788
Old Line State
Motto: Manly Deeds, Womanly Words
Tree: White Oak
Bird: Baltimore Oriole
Flower: Black-eyed Susan

Design Element & Order to Stitch	DMC® Embroidery Floss	Notes for Stitching
1. Date	921 Copper	Stitch the date inside the pattern lines using one strand of thread.
2. State Name	921 Copper	Outline and fill letters.
3. State Sillhouette	813 Blue, light	Outline state and fill.
4. Black-eyed Susans (leaves)	3011 Khaki Green, dark (outline/fill) 94 Khaki Green, variegated (veins)	Stitch veins. Outline and fill leaves.
5. Black-eyed Susans (flowers)	610 Drab Brown, dark (centers) 310 Black (centers) 111 Mustard, variegated (petals)	Thread needle with one strand black and one strand brown. Stitch flower centers. Outline and fill petals.
6. White Oak	3346 Hunter Green (leaf outline/fill) 94 Khaki Green, variegated (veins/acorn bottom) 610 Drab Brown, dark (acorn top	Stitch leaf veins. Outline and fill leaf. Stitch bottom portion of acorn. Stitch top of acorn.
7. Baltimore Oriole	310 Black (head, back, wing) White (feather tips) 921 Copper (breast) 648 Beaver Gray, light (eye, legs, beak)	Outline and fill solid black areas on head and back. Stitch white lines on tail and wing, and then fill around the white with black. Stitch the eye, legs and beak.

MASSACHUSETTS

Entered Union: February 6, 1788
Bay State
Motto: By the Sword We Seek Peace,
But Peace Only Under Liberty
Tree: American Elm
Bird: Black-capped Chickadee
Flower: Mayflower

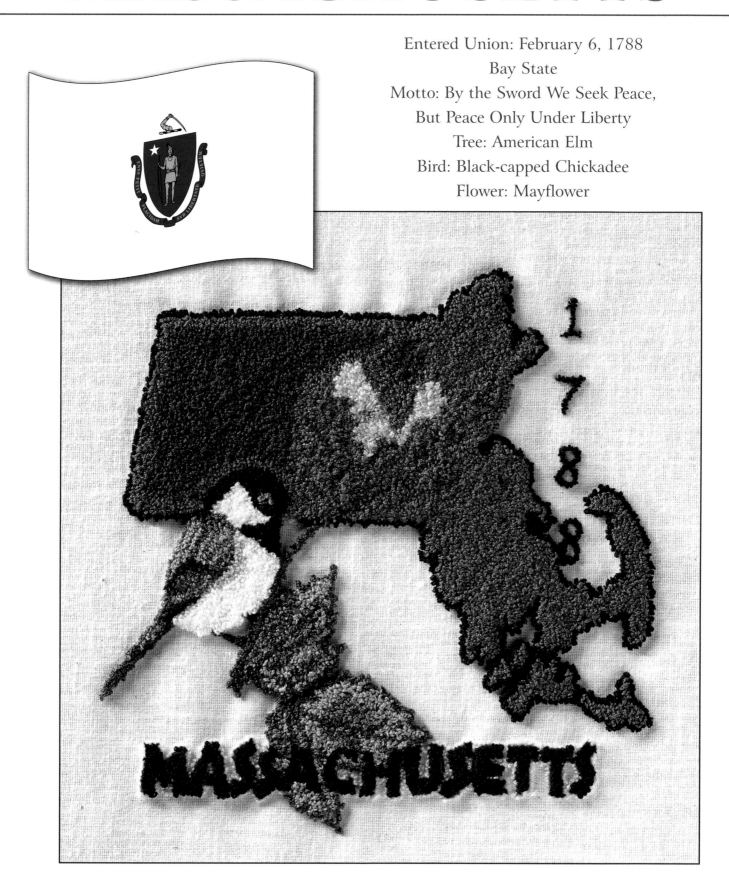

Design Element & Order to Stitch	DMC® Embroidery Floss	Notes for Stitching
1. State Sillhouette	3858 Burgundy, light (fill) 3857 Burgundy, medium (outline)	Outline state and fill.
2. Mayflower (leaves/stems)	936 Khaki Green, dark (veins/stems) 469 Khaki Green, medium (leaf fill) 3011 Khaki Brown (leaf fill)	Stitch veins and stems. Fill leaves with two shades of green.
3. Mayflower	948 Pink, light (petals) 48 Pink, variegated (petals) 3821 Yellow (centers)	Stitch all light pink areas first. Stitch darker areas with variegated pink. Add centers with one-strand needle and floss.
4. American Elm	936 Khaki Green, dark (veins/stems) 936/733/3011 Greens (leaf fill)	Stitch veins and stems. Fill leaves with mix of three green shades.
5. State Name	310 Black (outline/fill) 3823 Ivory (outline)	Outline and fill letters with two strands black. Adjust depth gauge to 1/4-inch loop length in three-strand needle and outline letters with ivory.
6. Date	310 Black	Adjust depth gauge to 3/16-inch loop length in one-strand needle. Stitch the date directly on the pattern lines.
7. Black-capped Chickadee	310 Black (feet, legs, head); 5200 White (head) 3031 Brown (stem/tail) 111 Gold, variegated (beak) 830/612/610/3031 Brown shades (back/wing) 3821 Yellow (beneath wing) 5200 White (breast)	Stitch legs and feet on pattern lines. Stitch and fill stem. Stitch head in black and white, and then add beak. Add tail. Work back and wing in shades of brown (refer to photo.) Add two rows of yellow beneath the wing, and then stitch breast in white.

MICHIGAN

Entered Union: January 26, 1837
The Wolverine State/Great Lakes State
Motto: If You Seek a Pleasant Peninsula,
Look About You
Tree: White Pine
Bird: Robin
Flower: Apple Blossom

Design Element & Order to Stitch	DMC® Embroidery Floss	Notes for Stitching
1. Date	921 Copper	Adjust depth gauge to 3/16-inch loop length in one-strand needle to outline and fill date.
2. State Name	921 Copper	Use one-strand needle with gauge set to 3/16-inch loop length to outline and fill letters.
3. State Sillhouette	930 Antique Blue, dark (2 skeins)	Outline state and fill.
4. Apple Blossoms (leave/stems)	610 Drab Brown, dark (stems/veins) 935 Avocado Green, dark (leaf outline/fill)	Stitch veins and stem. Outline and fill leaves.
5. Apple Blossoms (flowers)	90 Yellow, variegated (centers) 524 Fern Green, light (lines) 335 Rose (petal blush) BLANC (petals)	Stitch centers of flowers. Add lines that divide petals and stitch pink and white petals of each flower.
6. White Pine	3371 Black Brown (trunk/branches) 730 Olive Green, dark (foliage) 520 Fern Green, dark (foliage)	Stitch tree trunk and branches. Add pine needle foliage in two shades of green.
7. Robin	947 Burnt Orange (breast) BLANC (lower breast, top of leg, eye, feathers) 3371 Black Brown (head, back, wing, feathers) 3862 Mocha Beige, dark (back, wing feathers, feet) 111 Mustard, variegated (beak)	Stitch breast. Outline head, back and wing, and fill dark areas of wing feathers with darkest brown. Add white and lighter brown to fill in feathers on wings. Stitch white area at bottom of breast, eye and top of leg. Stitch and fill feet. Fill head and add beak

MINNESOTA

Entered Union: May 11, 1858
North Star State
Motto: The Star of the North
Tree: Red Pine
Bird: Common Loon
Flower: Pink and White Lady Slipper

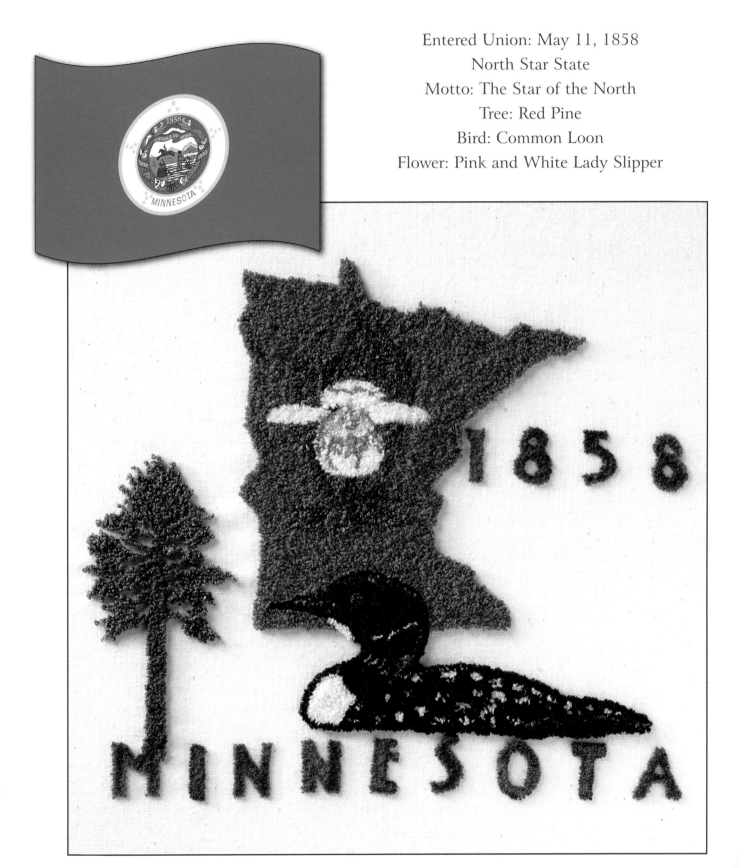

Design Element & Order to Stitch	DMC® Embroidery Floss	Notes for Stitching
1. Date	115 Garnet, variegated **(2 skeins)**	Adjust depth gauge to 3/16-inch loop length in one-strand needle to outline and fill date.
2. State Name	115 Garnet, variegated	Use one-strand needle with gauge set to 3/16-inch loop length to outline and fill letters.
3. Lady Slipper (leaves)	500 Blue Green, dark (veins, stem, outline) 520 Fern Green, dark (leaf fill) 730 Olive Green, dark (leaf fill)	Stitch veins and stem. Outline leaves. Use two shades of green to fill leaves.
4. Lady Slipper (flower)	107 Carnation, variegated (lines/center) BLANC White (petal fill) 725 Topaz (center)	Stitch pink lines. Add topaz and pink to throat/stamen, and add a few highlights of white. Fill petals.
5. Common Loon	BLANC White (spots, accents, breast, neck) 310 Black (body, head, outline) 53 Steel Gray, variegated (highlights) 433 Brown, medium (eye)	Stitch outline. Add spots on back, neck and head in white. Fill breast and neck areas in white. Add gray highlights on beak, head and neck. Add small round eye in brown and fill all remaining areas with black.
6. Red Pine	433 Brown, medium (trunk/limbs) 469 Avocado Green (foliage) 730 Olive Green, dark (foliage)	Stitch trunk and limbs. Stitch pine foliage using both shades of green to create shadow and light areas.
7. State Silhouette	355 Terra Cotta, dark **(2 skeins)**	Outline state perimeter. Outline around lady slipper and loon's head. Continue adding rows to fill state silhouette.

MISSISSIPPI

Entered Union: December 10, 1817
Magnolia State
Motto: By Valor and Arms
Tree: Magnolia
Bird: Mockingbird
Flower: Magnolia

Design Element & Order to Stitch	DMC® Embroidery Floss	Notes for Stitching
1. Date	3816 Celadon Green	Adjust depth gauge to 3/8-inch loop length in three-strand needle. Stitch the date just inside pattern lines. Fill numbers.
2. State Name	3816 Celadon Green	Outline and fill letters.
3. Magnolia (tree)	8299 Golden Olive, dark (trunk) 319 Pistachio Green, dark (foliage) 3011 Khaki Green, dark (foliage)	Stitch trunk. Thread needle with one strand of each green and fill foliage area.
4. Magnolia (leaves)	829 Golden Olive, dark (veins) 3011 Khaki Green, dark (leaf outline/fill)	Stitch veins. Outline and fill leaves.
5. Magnolia (petals)	BLANC (outline/fill) 3823 Ultra Pale Yellow (division shadows) 728 Topaz (center) 90 Yellow, variegated (center)	Outline petals. Add division shadows. Stitch dark oval at base of center using topaz. Add center in variegated yellow. Fill remaining petal areas.
6. Mockingbird	310 Black (beak, eye, leg) 610 Drab Brown, dark (outline/body) 3032 Mocha Brown, medium (markings) BLANC (outline, throat, breast, markings)	Outline head, back and tail with two rows of lighter brown. Outline and fill throat and breast with white. Add beak, eye and leg. Stitch white and darker brown feather and head markings. Fill remaining body area.
7. State Silhouette	991 Aquamarine, dark (3 skeins)	Outline and fill state silhouette. Take care not to snag the loops on the front design when stitching around completed elements.

MISSOURI

Entered Union: August 10, 1821
Show Me State
Motto: The Welfare of the People
Shall Be the Supreme Law
Tree: Flowering Dogwood
Bird: Eastern Bluebird
Flower: White Hawthorn Blossom

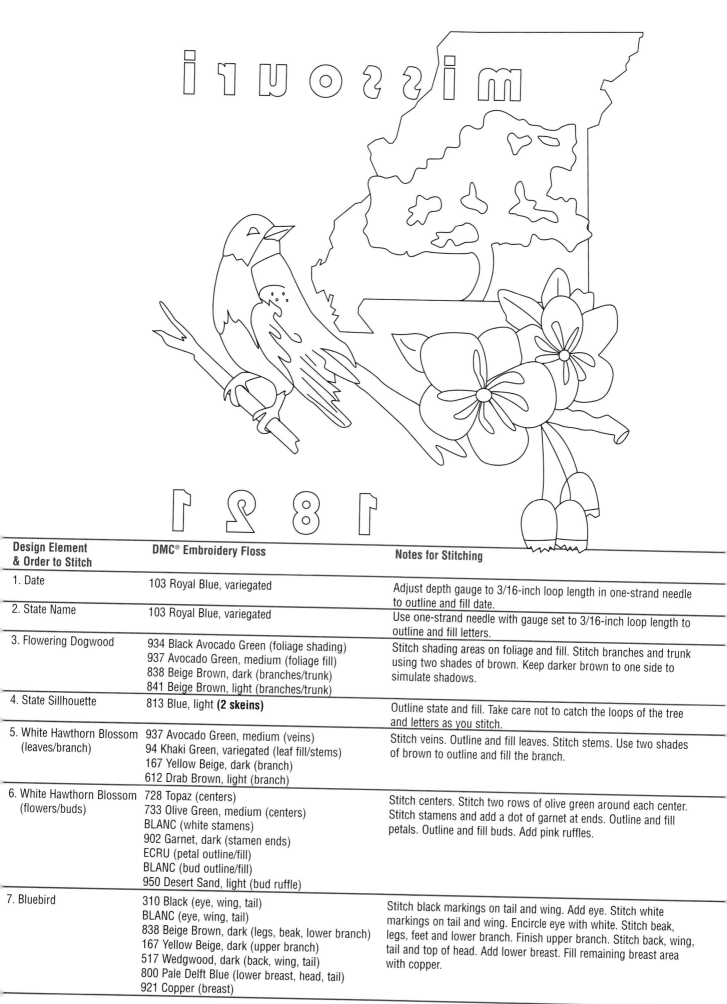

Design Element & Order to Stitch	DMC® Embroidery Floss	Notes for Stitching
1. Date	103 Royal Blue, variegated	Adjust depth gauge to 3/16-inch loop length in one-strand needle to outline and fill date.
2. State Name	103 Royal Blue, variegated	Use one-strand needle with gauge set to 3/16-inch loop length to outline and fill letters.
3. Flowering Dogwood	934 Black Avocado Green (foliage shading) 937 Avocado Green, medium (foliage fill) 838 Beige Brown, dark (branches/trunk) 841 Beige Brown, light (branches/trunk)	Stitch shading areas on foliage and fill. Stitch branches and trunk using two shades of brown. Keep darker brown to one side to simulate shadows.
4. State Sillhouette	813 Blue, light (2 skeins)	Outline state and fill. Take care not to catch the loops of the tree and letters as you stitch.
5. White Hawthorn Blossom (leaves/branch)	937 Avocado Green, medium (veins) 94 Khaki Green, variegated (leaf fill/stems) 167 Yellow Beige, dark (branch) 612 Drab Brown, light (branch)	Stitch veins. Outline and fill leaves. Stitch stems. Use two shades of brown to outline and fill the branch.
6. White Hawthorn Blossom (flowers/buds)	728 Topaz (centers) 733 Olive Green, medium (centers) BLANC (white stamens) 902 Garnet, dark (stamen ends) ECRU (petal outline/fill) BLANC (bud outline/fill) 950 Desert Sand, light (bud ruffle)	Stitch centers. Stitch two rows of olive green around each center. Stitch stamens and add a dot of garnet at ends. Outline and fill petals. Outline and fill buds. Add pink ruffles.
7. Bluebird	310 Black (eye, wing, tail) BLANC (eye, wing, tail) 838 Beige Brown, dark (legs, beak, lower branch) 167 Yellow Beige, dark (upper branch) 517 Wedgwood, dark (back, wing, tail) 800 Pale Delft Blue (lower breast, head, tail) 921 Copper (breast)	Stitch black markings on tail and wing. Add eye. Stitch white markings on tail and wing. Encircle eye with white. Stitch beak, legs, feet and lower branch. Finish upper branch. Stitch back, wing, tail and top of head. Add lower breast. Fill remaining breast area with copper.

MONTANA

Entered Union: November 8, 1889
Treasure State
Motto: Gold and Silver
Tree: Ponderosa Pine
Bird: Western Meadowlark
Flower: Bitterroot

Design Element & Order to Stitch	DMC® Embroidery Floss	Notes for Stitching
1. Date	902 Garnet, dark **(2 skeins)**	Adjust depth gauge to 3/16-inch loop length in one-strand needle to outline and then fill date.
2. State Name	902 Garnet, dark	Use one-strand needle with gauge set to 3/16-inch loop length to outline and fill letters.
3. State Silhouette	902 Garnet, dark (outline) 950 Desert Sand, light (fill) **(2 skeins)**	Outline state and fill.
4. Bitterroot (leaves/stem)	520 Fern Green, dark (veins/outlines) 937 Avocado Green, medium (fill/stem)	Stitch veins and outline. Fill leaves and stem.
5. Bitterroot (petals)	111 Mustard, variegated (centers) 902 Garnet, dark (petal lines) 52 Violet, variegated (petals)	Stitch centers. Add lines and fill petals.
6. Ponderosa Pine	420 Hazelnut Brown, dark (trunk) 838 Beige Brown, dark (branches/shade trunk) 520 Fern Green, dark (foliage) 934 Black Avocado Green (foliage)	Stitch trunk and branches. Add shade to one side of trunk. Stitch pine needle foliage in two shades of green, keeping darker green to bottoms of each branch cluster.
7. Western Meadowlark	728 Topaz (breast, throat, top of head) 310 Black (wing, eye, back) BLANC White (fill wing, back, head) 420 Hazelnut Brown, dark (legs/feet)	Stitch breast and throat. Outline head and back. Add black lines, eye and markings. Add topaz to top of head. Fill remaining areas in white. Stitch legs and feet.
8. Stump (perch)	300 Mahogany, medium (fill) 838 Beige Brown, dark (stump lines)	Stitch lines in stump, and then fill.

NEBRASKA

Entered Union: March 1, 1867
Cornhusker State
Motto: Equality Before the Law
Tree: Cottonwood
Bird: Western Meadowlark
Flower: Goldenrod

Design Element & Order to Stitch	DMC® Embroidery Floss	Notes for Stitching
1. Date	90 Yellow, variegated	Adjust depth gauge to 3/16-inch loop length in one-strand needle to outline and fill date.
2. State Name	728 Topaz 3760 Wedgewood, medium	Use three-strand needle with gauge set to 3/8-inch loop length. Thread needle with one strand of each color. Outline and fill letters.
3. Cottonwood	898 Coffee Brown, dark (trunk/branches) 730 Olive Green, dark (foliage) 520 Fern Green, dark (foliage)	Outline and fill trunk and branches. Outline and fill foliage with greens; use lighter green to create highlights in the foliage.
4. Western Meadowlark	310 Black (beak, throat, eye) 610 Drab Brown, dark (feathers) 898 Coffee Brown, dark (head, back, under tail) 728 Topaz (breast/throat) BLANC (feathers, beak, head)	Outline top of head, back and under tail with coffee brown. Outline and fill breast and throat with topaz. Stitch black at top of beak, throat and eye. Use white and lighter brown to stitch feathers. Use white to fill beak and top of head.
5. Goldenrod (leaves/stem)	730 Olive Green, dark (veins) 520 Fern Green, dark (fill/stem)	Stitch veins in darker green. Stitch stem. Outline and fill leaves in lighter green.
6. Goldenrod (petals)	90 Yellow, variegated	Outline and fill flower head.
7. State Silhouette	3760 Wedgewood, medium (2 skeins)	Outline and fill state silhouette. Take care stitching around completed elements; do not snag their loops on the front of the design.

NEVADA

Entered Union: October 31, 1864
Sagebrush State/Silver State
Motto: All For Our Country
Tree: Single-leaf Pinon
Bird: Mountain Bluebird
Flower: Sagebrush

Design Element & Order to Stitch	DMC® Embroidery Floss	Notes for Stitching
1. Date	300 Mahogany, dark	Adjust depth gauge to 5/16-inch loop length in one-strand needle. Outline the date using one or two strands. Fill numbers.
2. State Name	300 Mahogany, dark	Use one-strand needle to outline and fill letters using one or two strands.
3. Single-leaf Pine	830 Golden Olive, dark (branch) 500 Blue Green (pine needles) 524 Fern Green, light (pine needle highlights) 830 Golden Olive, dark (pinecone outline) 372 Mustard, light (pinecone fill)	Stitch pine branch using two rows. Add pine needles using one row for each needle. Add some highlights to a few pine needles toward the end of the branch. Stitch outline and crosshatching on pinecone. Fill each area.
4. Sagebrush	320 Pistachio Green, medium (stem/leaves) 3364 Pine Green (leaves) 111 Mustard, variegated (flowers)	Stitch stem with two rows. Add leaves using a combination of each green. Keep the darker green to the outside of each leaf. Outline and fill the flowers.
5. Mountain Bluebird	103 Royal Blue, variegated (outline) 931 Antique Blue, medium (head/wing fill) 310 Black (eye/legs) BLANC (lower breast) 921 Copper (upper breast) 728 Topaz (beak)	Stitch outline of head, back, tail and wing in variegated blue. Add lines on wing in variegated blue. Fill head and wing. Add eye and legs. Stitch beak in topaz. Fill lower portion of breast and then upper portion.
6. Bird's Perch	3371 Black Brown (center hole of perch) 829 Golden Olive, very dark (fill) 642 Beige Gray, dark (highlights)	Stitch outline of dark hole in center of tree perch. Fill. Add some vertical lines with dark brown. Fill outward, adding on the inner areas and around the edges.
7. State Silhouette	3853 Autumn Gold, dark 3776 Desert Sand, medium 301 Mahogany, medium **(1 skein each)**	Thread three-strand needle with one yard of a copper shade. Outline state silhouette. When thread is depleted, thread needle with one yard of next shade of copper and continue outlining. Continue in this manner until outline is complete. Move inside row, and continue as before. Completely fill the silhouette with this technique (see photo). Fill small areas with one color.

NEW HAMPSHIRE

Entered Union: June 21, 1788
Granite State
Motto: Live Free or Die
Tree: White Birch
Bird: Purple Finch
Flower: Purple Lilac

Design Element & Order to Stitch	DMC® Embroidery Floss	Notes for Stitching
1. Date	115 Garnet, variegated	Adjust depth gauge to 5/16-inch loop length in one-strand needle to outline and fill date.
2. State Name	115 Garnet, variegated	Use one-strand needle to outline and fill letters.
3. White Birch	648 Beaver Gray, light (trunk/limbs) 898 Coffee Brown, dark (trunk lines) 890 Pistachio Green, dark (foliage fill) 935 Avocado Green, dark (foliage outline	Stitch most of trunk and limbs with light gray. Add small horizontal lines of dark brown. Outline foliage area and fill patches of the area with the same green. Fill remaining open areas.
4. Lilac (leaves/stem)	502 Blue Green (fill) 500 Blue Green, dark (outline, veins, stem)	Outline leaves. Add veins and shadows. Fill other areas. Add stem.
5. Lilac (petals)	3041 Antique Violet, medium (petals) 327 Violet, dark (petals) 316 Antique Mauve, medium (petals)	Stitch tiny petals using all three violet colors; use more of the darkest, then the medium, and then the lightest value. Leave some open areas to add an airy feel to the flower head.
6. Purple Finch	115 Garnet, variegated (outline, head/throat fill) 3777 Terra Cotta, dark 948 Peach, light (breast outline/fill) 3023 Brown Gray, light (breast) 310 Black (beak, eye, legs, markings)	Stitch outline across top of head and down back to just above tail. Add beak, eye and legs. Add markings across wing and back. Fill head and throat. Outline and fill breast and add markings across wings. Add light gray areas on breast. Fill remaining areas with terra cotta.
7. State Silhouette	728 Topaz (**2 skeins**)	Outline and fill state.

NEW JERSEY

Entered Union: December 18, 1787
Garden State
Motto: Liberty and Prosperity
Tree: Northern Red Oak
Bird: Eastern Goldfinch
Flower: Violet

Design Element & Order to Stitch	DMC® Embroidery Floss	Notes for Stitching
1. Date	336 Navy Blue	Adjust depth gauge to 5/16-inch loop length in one-strand needle, to outline and fill date.
2. State Name	336 Navy Blue	Use one-strand needle to outline and fill letters using one-two strands.
3. Red Oak (leaf/acorn)	3364 Pine Green (veins) 935 Avocado Green, dark (leaf outline/fill) 830 Golden Olive, dark (acorn caps/crosshatch) 733 Olive Green, medium (acorn fill/bottom outline)	Stitch veins in single rows. Outline and fill leaf. Outline acorn caps and crosshatched lines. Fill. Outline acorn bottom. Add shadow in darker color.
4. Violet	336 Navy (outline/lines) 161 Gray Blue (lower petals fill) 168 Pewter, very light (upper petals fill/outline) 830 Golden Olive, dark (center)	Outline center, lower petals and add lines in navy. Outline and fill upper petals. Fill lower petals. Stitch center.
5. Eastern Goldfinch	728 Topaz 310 Black BLANC	Outline and fill topaz portions of finch. Stitch white areas of wing and tail. Outline and fill white area beneath tail. Stitch eye and beak and highlight with white. Outline and fill black on head, beak, wing and tail.
6. State Silhouette	937 Avocado Green, medium 3364 Pine Green 471 Avocado Green, light 3011 Khaki Green, dark **(1 skein each)**	Thread three-strand needle with one yard (three strands) of any green shade. Outline state silhouette. When thread is depleted, thread needle with one yard of next shade of green and continue outlining. Continue with next two shades. When initial outline is complete, move to inside that row, and continue stitching as before. Use this technique to fill the silhouette. Fill small areas with one color (see photo).

NEW MEXICO

Entered Union: January 6, 1912
Land of Enchantment
Motto: It Grows As It Goes
Tree: Pinon
Bird: Roadrunner
Flower: Yucca

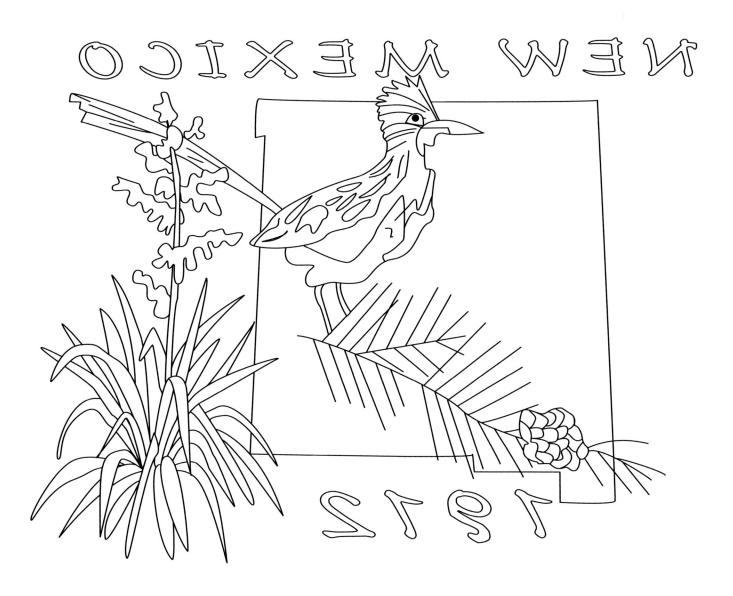

Design Element & Order to Stitch	DMC® Embroidery Floss	Notes for Stitching
1. Date	356 Terra Cotta, medium	Adjust depth gauge to 5/16-inch loop length in one-strand needle to outline and fill date.
2. State Name	356 Terra Cotta, medium	Use one-strand needle to outline and fill letters.
3. Pinon	500 Blue Green, dark (pine needles) 830 Golden Olive, dark (stems, limb, outline, fill) 612 Drab Brown, light (pinecone outline/fill)	Stitch stems and main limb using one row. Stitch each pine needle with one row. Use golden olive and brown to outline and fill sections of pinecone.
4. Yucca	320 Pistachio Green, medium (leaf outline/fill) 524 Fern Green, light (leaf highlight) 830 Golden Olive, dark (stem) 745 Pale Yellow, light (flowers)	Outline leaves and fill all but a small slice where a highlight will be placed. Use lighter green to fill highlight area on most leaves. Stitch stem with two rows. Stitch the irregular shaped flowers along main stem.
5. Roadrunner	3371 Black Brown (head, body, tail outline) 838 Beige Brown, dark (breast top, body, tail) 310 Black (beak, eye, legs) 3047 Yellow Beige, light (breast fill/throat)	Outline head, body and tail. Outline and fill top area of breast. Stitch lines on head and body in beige brown. Add lines to the tail. Outline and fill breast. Fill small light area on throat. Stitch beak, eye and legs.
6. State Silhouette	502 Blue Green (3 skeins)	Outline and fill state. Take care not to catch loops of design elements already punched in that space.

NEW YORK

Entered Union: July 26, 1788
Empire State
Motto: Excelsior – Ever Upward
Tree: Sugar Maple
Bird: Eastern Bluebird
Flower: Rose

Design Element & Order to Stitch	DMC® Embroidery Floss	Notes for Stitching
1. Date	315 Antique Mauve, medium (fill) 48 Baby Pink, variegated (highlight)	Adjust depth gauge to 5/16-inch loop length in one-strand needle to outline and fill date using one or two strands. Add highlight against left side of numbers inside state silhouette.
2. State Name	315 Antique Mauve, dark	Use one-strand needle with gauge set to 3/16-inch loop length to outline and fill letters using one or two strands.
3. Sugar Maple	610 Drab Brown, dark (trunk/branches) 470 Avocado Green, light (foliage outline/fill)	Stitch trunk and branches. Outline and fill foliage.
4. Rose	3722 Shell Pink, medium (petal outline) 48 Baby Pink, variegated (petal fill) 335 Rose (petal fill)	Outline each rose petal. Fill petals with variegated pink to highlight, and rose to complete each petal.
5. Eastern Bluebird	103 Royal Blue, variegated (outline/wing lines) 931 Antique Blue, medium (head/wing fill) 921 Copper (upper breast) 310 Black (eye/legs) BLANC (lower breast)	Stitch outline of head, back, tail and wing. Add lines on wing. Fill head and wing. Add eye and legs; add eye highlight in white. Fill lower portion of breast, and then upper portion.
6. State Silhouette	3721 Shell Pink, dark (2 skeins)	Outline and fill state. Take care as you stitch around the bird and numbers; do not catch the punched loops.

NORTH CAROLINA

Entered Union: November 21, 1789
Tarheel State/Old North State
Motto: To Be Rather Than To Seem
Tree: Pine
Bird: Cardinal
Flower: American Dogwood

Design Element & Order to Stitch	DMC® Embroidery Floss	Notes for Stitching
1. Date	115 Scarlet, variegated	Adjust depth gauge to 5/16-inch loop length in one-strand needle to outline and fill date using one or two strand.
2. State Name	890 Pistachio Green, dark	Use one-strand needle with gauge set to 5/16-inch loop length to outline and fill letters using one or two strands.
3. Pine	838 Beige Brown, dark (branch, pinecone outline) 420 Hazelnut Brown, dark (branch, pinecone fill) 105 Tan/Brown, variegated (pinecone) 935 Avocado Green, dark (needles) 937 Avocado Green, medium (needles) 3364 Pine Green (needles)	Use one strand darkest brown to stitch along branch and stem pattern lines. Shade and highlight branches and stems using lighter brown and variegated tans. Use one strand lighter brown to outline pinecone. Stitch pinecone lines using one strand tan. Fill in open areas with darkest brown. Use two strands medium green to stitch pine needle lines. Highlight and shade pine needles with mixture of greens.
4. American Dogwood	111 Mustard, variegated (center outline/fill) 733 Olive Green, medium (dots) 420 Hazelnut Brown, dark (petal tip shadows) 648 Beaver Gray, light (petal shadows) BLANC (petal fill)	Outline and fill centers with one strand. Add small dots. Use two strands to create shadows on petal tips. Use two strands to create shadow lines on and between petals. Fill petals with two strands.
5. Cardinal	51 Burnt Orange, variegated (legs, eye, beak) 310 Black (face) 321 Red (body) 349 Coral, dark (wing lines/tail) 838 Beige Brown, dark (branch) 420 Hazelnut Brown, dark (branch) 105 Tan/Brown, variegated (branch)	Stitch beak, eye and legs using one strand. Use two strandsl to stitch along wing lines and beneath tail. Fill remaining areas of body. Stitch branch on pattern line using dark brown, then lighter brown. Highlight with variegated tans.
6. State Silhouette	890 Pistachio Green, dark **(2 skeins)**	Outline and fill state with green.

NORTH DAKOTA

Entered Union: November 2, 1889
Peace Garden State
Motto: Liberty and Union, Now and Forever
Tree: American Elm
Bird: Western Meadowlark
Flower: Wild Prairie Rose

Design Element & Order to Stitch	DMC® Embroidery Floss	Notes for Stitching
1. Date	926 Gray Green, medium	Adjust depth gauge to 5/16-inch loop length in one-strand needle to outline and fill date using one or two strands.
2. State Name	926 Gray Green, medium	Use one-strand needle with gauge set to 5/16-inch loop length to outline and fill letters using one or two strands.
3. American Elm	934 Black Avocado Green (veins) 3364 Pine Green (leaf fill)	Using one strand, stitch two rows to create leaf veins. Outline and fill leaves with two strands.
4. Wild Prairie Rose (leaves)	3364 Pine Green (veins) 937 Avocado Green, medium (leaf fill)	Stitch veins using one. Outline and fill leaves using two strands.
5. Wild Prairie Rose (flowers)	915 Plum, dark (outline/shadows) 107 Carnation, variegated (petal fill) 90 Yellow, variegated (centers)	Use two strands to outline and create shadows between petals. Fill petals with two strands. Outline and fill centers.
6. Western Meadowlark	3023 Brown Gray, light (beak) 310 Black (eye) 90 Yellow, variegated (legs) ECRU (head/wing fill) 3371 Black Brown (wing markings) 3820 Straw, dark (breast/throat)	Using one strand of thread, stitch beak, eye and legs using colors indicated. Use two strands to stitch markings on wing. Fill areas of head and wing. Fill remaining areas of breast and throat.
7. Tree Stump	645 Beaver Gray, dark 3023 Brown Gray, light 642 Beige Gray, dark 3866 Mocha Brown, light	To create the old stump, use darker shades of beiges and grays to stitch irregular, vertical strips closest to the leaves. Gradually stitch lighter shades as you go away from the leaves (see photo).
8. State Silhouette	3750 Antique Blue, dark (2 skeins)	Outline and fill state. Take care as you stitch around the other design elements so you do not catch the punched loops.

OHIO

Entered Union: March 1, 1803
Buckeye State
Motto: With God, All Things are Possible
Tree: Ohio Buckeye
Bird: Cardinal
Flower: Scarlet Carnation

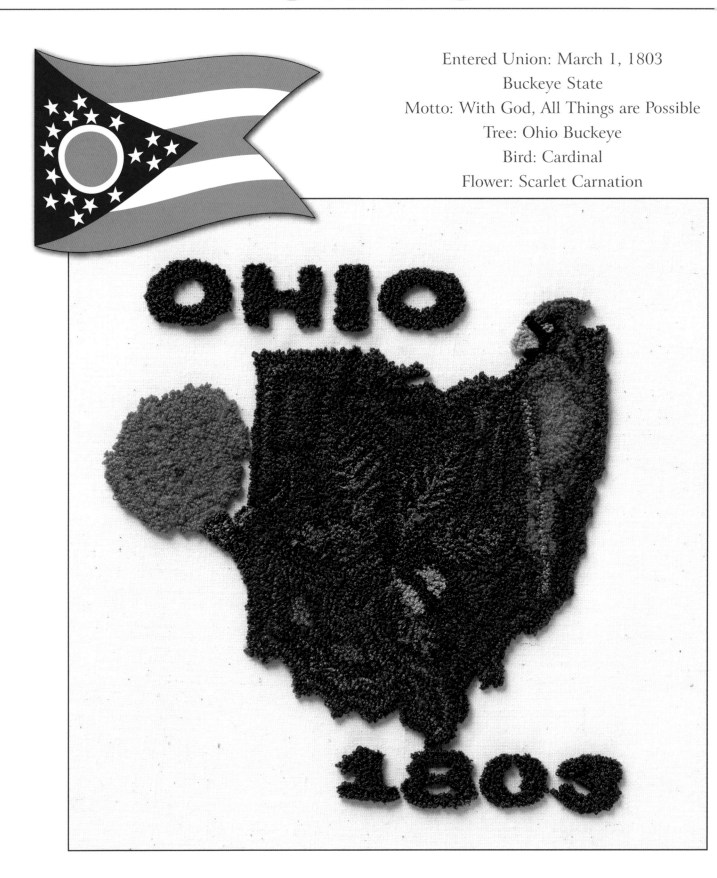

Design Element & Order to Stitch	DMC® Embroidery Floss	Notes for Stitching
1. Date	336 Navy Blue	Adjust depth gauge to 5/16-inch loop length in one-strand needle to outline and fill date using one or two strands.
2. State Name	336 Navy Blue	Use one-strand needle with gauge set to 5/16-inch loop length to outline and fill letters using one or two strands.
3. Ohio Buckeye	935 Avocado Green, dark (leaf outline/fill) 937 Avocado Green, medium (leaf veins) 938 Coffee Brown, dark (leaf stem/buckeye fill) 3828 Hazelnut Brown (eye of buckeye) 612 Drab Brown, light (highlight on buckeye)	Stitch veins using one strand. Stitch stem using two strands. Outline and fill leaves with two strands. Use two strands to stitch highlight and eye of buckeye. Outline and fill buckeye nut.
4. Carnation (leaves/stems)	3363 Pine Green, medium (leaf/stem highlights) 520 Fern Green, dark (leaf/stems)	Stitch highlights on stem and leaf. Outline and fill stem and leaf.
5. Carnation (flower)	115 Scarlet, variegated (outline, petal lines, fill) 349 Coral, dark (flower fill) 321 Red (flower fill)	Stitch outline of flower and on lines of petals. Fill flower with variety of reds, keeping lights against darks to create contrast and depth.
6. Cardinal	51 Burnt Orange, variegated (legs, eye, beak) 115 Scarlet, variegated (outline, body, tail) 310 Black (face) 349 Coral, dark (body) 347 Salmon, dark (wing, face) 321 Red (body) 938 Coffee Brown, dark (branch) 420 Hazelnut Brown, dark (branch)	Stitch beak, eye and legs using one strand. Use two strands of variegated scarlet to stitch outline along top of head, back, and left wing. Refer to photo and stitch darkest red areas using two strands. Fill body using light and medium reds on head and breast. Outline and fill tail. Stitch branch on pattern line using dark brown, and then lighter brown.
7. State Silhouette	103 Royal Blue, variegated **(2 skeins)**	Outline and fill state. Take care not to catch the punched loops.

OKLAHOMA

Entered Union: November 16, 1907
Sooner State
Motto: Labor Conquers All Things
Tree: Redbud
Bird: Scissor-tailed Flycatcher
Flower: Mistletoe

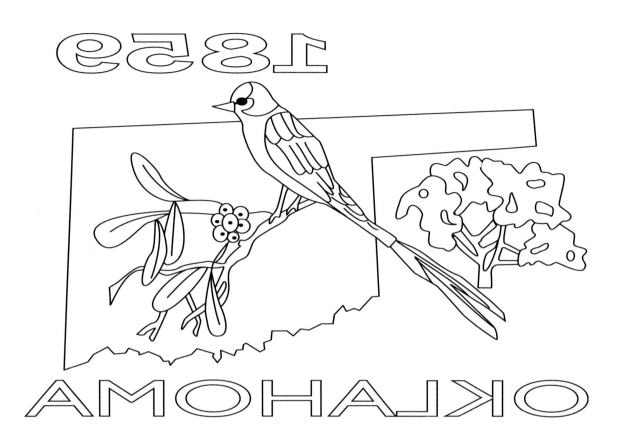

Design Element & Order to Stitch	DMC® Embroidery Floss	Notes for Stitching
1. Date	732 Olive Green	Adjust depth gauge to 5/16-inch loop length in one-strand needle to outline and fill date using one or two strands.
2. State Name	732 Olive Green	Use one-strand needle with gauge set to 5/16-inch loop length to outline and fill letters using one or two strands.
3. Redbud	3031 Mocha Brown, dark (trunk/branches) 917 Plum, medium (foliage) 733 Olive Green, medium (foliage)	Outline and fill trunk and tree branches. Using one strand each of plum and olive green in the needle together, outline and fill the foliage areas of the tree.
4. Mistletoe (leaves/stems)	610 Drab Brown, dark (stems) 3347 Yellow Green, medium (leaves)	Stitch stems using two strands. Outline and fill leaves.
5. Mistletoe (berries)	371 Mustard (berries)	Stitch berries.
6. Scissor-tailed Flycatcher	961 Dusty Rose, dark (under wing area) 53 Steel Gray, variegated (head outline/fill, wings) 413 Pewter Gray, dark (wing lines) 310 Black (beak, eye, legs, tail) BLANC (head, breast, tail)	Stitch beak, eye and legs using one strand. Use two strands of black to stitch outline along top of back and length of tail. Create lines on wing. Fill areas between lines with variegated steel gray. Outline and fill head. Fill open areas of tail. Stitch a line under wing area. Fill breast with white.
7. State Silhouette	315 Antique Mauve (2 skeins)	Outline and fill state. Take care so you do not catch the punched loops.

OREGON

Entered Union: February 14, 1859
Beaver State
Motto: She Flies With Her Own Wings
Tree: Coastal Douglas Fir
Bird: Western Meadowlark
Flower: Oregon Grape

Design Element & Order to Stitch	DMC® Embroidery Floss	Notes for Stitching
1. Date	3808 Turquoise, dark	Adjust depth gauge to 5/16-inch loop length in one-strand needle to outline and fill date using one or two strands.
2. State Name	3808 Turquoise, dark	Use one-strand needle with gauge set to 5/16-inch loop length to outline and fill letters using one or two strands.
3. Coastal Douglas Fir	934 Black Avocado Green (shadows) 3345 Hunter Green, dark (tree fill)	Using two strands stitch beneath each section of pine boughs to create shadows. Fill the remaining areas of the tree.
4. Oregon Grape (leaves/stems)	371 Mustard (veins) 3345 Hunter Green, dark (leaves/stem)	Stitch veins in leaves using one strand. Stitch stem and fill leaves using two strands.
5. Oregon Grape (flowers)	3031 Mocha Brown, dark (shadows) 3826 Golden Brown (centers/division lines) 3821 Straw (petals)	Using one strand create shadows between petals. Stitch flower centers and division lines between petals using one strand. Fill petals with two strands.
6. Western Meadowlark	898 Coffee Brown, dark (beak, eye, legs, wing/breast markings) 3821 Straw (breast/throat fill) B5200 Snow White (head/wing fill)	Stitch beak, eye and legs using one strand. Use two strands to stitch markings on wing and breast. Fill areas of head and wing. Fill remaining areas of breast and throat.
7. State Silhouette	598 Turquoise, light (2 skeins)	Outline and fill state. Take care not to catch the punched loops.

PENNSYLVANIA

Entered Union: December 12, 1787
Keystone State
Motto: Virtue, Liberty, and Independence
Tree: Eastern Hemlock
Bird: Ruffed Grouse
Flower: Mountain Laurel

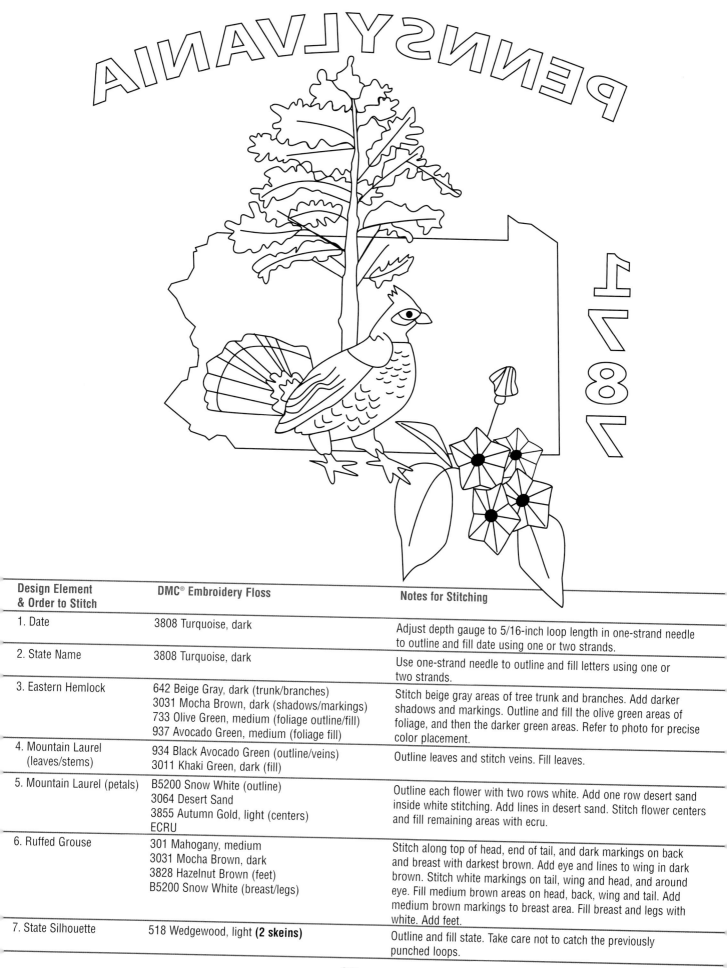

PENNSYLVANIA

1787

Design Element & Order to Stitch	DMC® Embroidery Floss	Notes for Stitching
1. Date	3808 Turquoise, dark	Adjust depth gauge to 5/16-inch loop length in one-strand needle to outline and fill date using one or two strands.
2. State Name	3808 Turquoise, dark	Use one-strand needle to outline and fill letters using one or two strands.
3. Eastern Hemlock	642 Beige Gray, dark (trunk/branches) 3031 Mocha Brown, dark (shadows/markings) 733 Olive Green, medium (foliage outline/fill) 937 Avocado Green, medium (foliage fill)	Stitch beige gray areas of tree trunk and branches. Add darker shadows and markings. Outline and fill the olive green areas of foliage, and then the darker green areas. Refer to photo for precise color placement.
4. Mountain Laurel (leaves/stems)	934 Black Avocado Green (outline/veins) 3011 Khaki Green, dark (fill)	Outline leaves and stitch veins. Fill leaves.
5. Mountain Laurel (petals)	B5200 Snow White (outline) 3064 Desert Sand 3855 Autumn Gold, light (centers) ECRU	Outline each flower with two rows white. Add one row desert sand inside white stitching. Add lines in desert sand. Stitch flower centers and fill remaining areas with ecru.
6. Ruffed Grouse	301 Mahogany, medium 3031 Mocha Brown, dark 3828 Hazelnut Brown (feet) B5200 Snow White (breast/legs)	Stitch along top of head, end of tail, and dark markings on back and breast with darkest brown. Add eye and lines to wing in dark brown. Stitch white markings on tail, wing and head, and around eye. Fill medium brown areas on head, back, wing and tail. Add medium brown markings to breast area. Fill breast and legs with white. Add feet.
7. State Silhouette	518 Wedgewood, light (2 skeins)	Outline and fill state. Take care not to catch the previously punched loops.

RHODE ISLAND

Entered Union: May 29, 1790
Ocean State
Motto: Hope
Tree: Red Maple
Bird: Rhode Island Red
Flower: Violet

Design Element & Order to Stitch	DMC® Embroidery Floss	Notes for Stitching
1. Date	947 Burnt Orange	Adjust depth gauge to 5/16-inch loop length in one-strand needle to outline and fill date using one or two strands.
2. State Name	947 Burnt Orange	Use one-strand needle to outline and fill letters using one or two strands.
3. Red Maple (leaf)	3064 Desert Sand (veins/stem) 947 Burnt Orange (fill) 350 Coral, medium (fill) 3826 Golden Brown (fill)	Stitch veins and stem on pattern lines. Fill leaf with colors in a patchwork-style technique. Refer to photo for approximate color placement.
4. Violet (leaves/stems)	319 Pistachio Green, dark (stems/outline) 3346 Hunter Green (fill)	Stitch flower stems on pattern line. Outline and fill shadowed areas of leaves with darker green. Fill leaves.
5. Violet (petals)	939 Navy Blue, dark (center surround) 793 Cornflower Blue, medium (outline/fill) 733 Olive Green, medium (centers)	Stitch navy blue surrounding flower centers and to slightly divide petals. Outline and fill petals. Add tiny centers.
6. Rhode Island Red	947 Burnt Orange (face/back) 350 Coral, medium (comb outline/fill, breast) 300 Mahogany, dark (back) 3826 Golden Brown (beak, neck feathers, legs) 3064 Desert Sand (breast) 310 Black (eye/tail feathers) 645 Beaver Gray, dark (tail feathers)	Stitch outline of comb and fill. Stitch face and fill. Stitch eye. Stitch beak, neck feathers, legs and feet. Add a small amount of orange along feet and legs to highlight. Using one strand black and one strand gray in the needle, stitch tail feathers. Using one strand of orange and one strand of brown in needle, stitch back. Using one strand of lighter brown and one strand of coral in needle, stitch breast.
7. State Silhouette	733 Olive Green, medium (2 skeins)	Outline and fill state. Take care not to catch the punched loops.

SOUTH CAROLINA

Entered Union: May 23, 1788
Palmetto State
Motto: While I Breathe, I Hope
Tree: Palmetto
Bird: Carolina Wren
Flower: Yellow Jessamine

Design Element & Order to Stitch	DMC® Embroidery Floss	Notes for Stitching
1. Date	902 Garnet, dark	Adjust depth gauge to 5/16-inch loop length in one-strand needle to outline and fill date using one or two strands.
2. State Name	902 Garnet, dark	Use one-strand needle to outline and fill letters using one or two strands.
3. Palmetto	3031 Mocha Brown, dark (trunk lines) 642 Beige Gray, dark (trunk fill) 500 Blue Green, dark (outline/lines) 937 Avocado Green, medium (fill)	Stitch jagged lines on tree trunk. Fill trunk. Stitch outline of each palmetto frond and on lines of each frond. Fill each frond.
4. Yellow Jessamine (leaves/stems)	934 Black Avocado Green (fill) 319 Pistachio Green, dark (veins)	Stitch veins along center of each leaf. Fill each leaf shape.
5. Yellow Jessamine (petals)	3821 Straw (centers/outline) 937 Avocado Green, medium (throats) 3855 Autumn Gold, light (fill)	Stitch centers. Stitch around and between each petal and throat of each flower with straw. Fill each petal. Add a small amount of green to center of flower throats.
6. Carolina Wren	3031 Mocha Brown, dark (outline) B5200 Snow White (wing/tail/head/eye markings) 3828 Hazelnut Brown (head, back, wing, tail fill, branch) 310 Black (eye, beak, branch) 3821 Straw (lower breast) ECRU (upper breast)	Stitch outline along top of head and lines on tail, wing and back. Add white area on head and around eye. Add white to wing and tail. Stitch eye and beak. Add a small amount of black to wing and tail. Fill remaining areas of wing, tail and back. Fill remainder of head. Stitch upper breast and lower breast. Add legs. Stitch branch using black and hazelnut brown.
7. State Silhouette	315 Dark Antique Mauve, medium (**2 skeins**) 902 Garnet, dark (optional)	Outline and fill state with mauve. Take care not to catch the punched loops. For added interest, add a few rows of the garnet.

SOUTH DAKOTA

Entered Union: November 2, 1889
Coyote State/Mount Rushmore State
Motto: Under God, the People Rule
Tree: Black Hills Spruce
Bird: Ring-necked Pheasant
Flower: American Pasque Flower

Design Element & Order to Stitch	DMC® Embroidery Floss	Notes for Stitching
1. Date	517 Wedgewood, dark	Adjust depth gauge to 5/16-inch loop length in one-strand needle to outline and fill date using one or two strands.
2. State Name	517 Wedgewood, dark	Use one-strand needle to outline and fill letters using one or two strands.
3. Black Hills Spruce	3031 Mocha Brown, dark (trunk) 934 Black Avocado Green (shadows) 3011 Khaki Green, dark (foliage)	Outline and fill trunk. Stitch shadowed areas beneath boughs. Add remaining foliage.
4. American Pasque Flower (leaves/stems)	500 Blue Green, dark (stems/veins) 3363 Pine Green, medium (leaf fill)	Outline stems and leaf veins. Fill leaves.
5. American Pasque Flower (petals)	3821 Straw 318 Steel Gray, light (outline) B5200 Snow White (fill)	Stitch straw areas of petals. Outline petals. Fill remaining petal areas.
6. Ring-necked Pheasant	350 Coral, medium (breast/comb) 500 Blue Green, dark (head/neck) B5200 Snow White (ring, wing, tail) 938 Coffee Brown, ultra dark (tail/wing markings, breast) 801 Coffee Brown, dark (wing, tail, back) 3828 Hazelnut Brown (eye, beak, legs, feet, wing, tail, back)	Stitch coral areas of breast and comb on head. Stitch eye and beak. Stitch blue green areas of head and neck. Add ring on neck. Stitch and fill white area on wing and beneath tail. Stitch legs and feet. Add markings on tail and wing. Outline and fill darker brown area of breast. Using one strand lighter brown and one strand darker brown in needle, fill in remaining areas of wing, tail and back.
7. State Silhouette	813 Blue, light (2 skeins)	Outline and fill state. Take care not to catch the punched loops.

TENNESSEE

Entered Union: June 1, 1796
Volunteer State
Motto: Agriculture and Commerce
Tree: Tulip Poplar
Bird: Mockingbird
Flower: Iris

Design Element & Order to Stitch	DMC® Embroidery Floss	Notes for Stitching
1. Date	111 Mustard, variegated	Adjust depth gauge to 5/16-inch loop length in one-strand needle to outline and fill date using one or two strands.
2. State Name	111 Mustard, variegated	Use one-strand needle to outline and fill letters using one or two strands.
3. Tulip Poplar	938 Coffee Brown, dark (trunk/branches) 3345 Hunter Green, dark (foliage)	Stitch tree trunk and branches using three-strand needle and two strands of thread. Stitch foliage.
4. Iris (leaves/stem)	3347 Yellow Green, medium (leaf outline/fill) 3345 Hunter Green, dark (stem)	Outline and fill leaves. Stitch stem.
5. Iris (petals)	111 Mustard, variegated 340 Blue Violet, medium (outline/fill) ECRU (fill)	Add mustard to each petal, stitching right on pattern lines. Outline each petal. Using one strand blue violet and one strand ecru in the needle fill the remaining areas of each petal.
6. Mockingbird and Branch	ECRU (wing lines, outer tail, breast) 610 Drab Brown, dark (branch outline/fill, wing, tail, beak) 642 Beige Gray, dark (head/back outline, fill) 310 Black (branch outline/fill, eye)	With one strand black and one strand drab brown in needle, outline and fill branch. Stitch on the wing lines and around the tail. Outline and fill breast areas. Fill in remaining areas of wing and tail using drab brown. Stitch beak. Stitch eye. Outline head and back and fill.
7. State Silhouette	920 Copper, medium 921 Copper **(2 skeins or 1 skein of each color)**	Outline and fill state with one or both shades copper. Take care not to catch the punched loops.

TEXAS

Entered Union: December 29, 1845
Lone Star State
Motto: Friendship
Tree: Pecan
Bird: Mockingbird
Flower: Bluebonnet

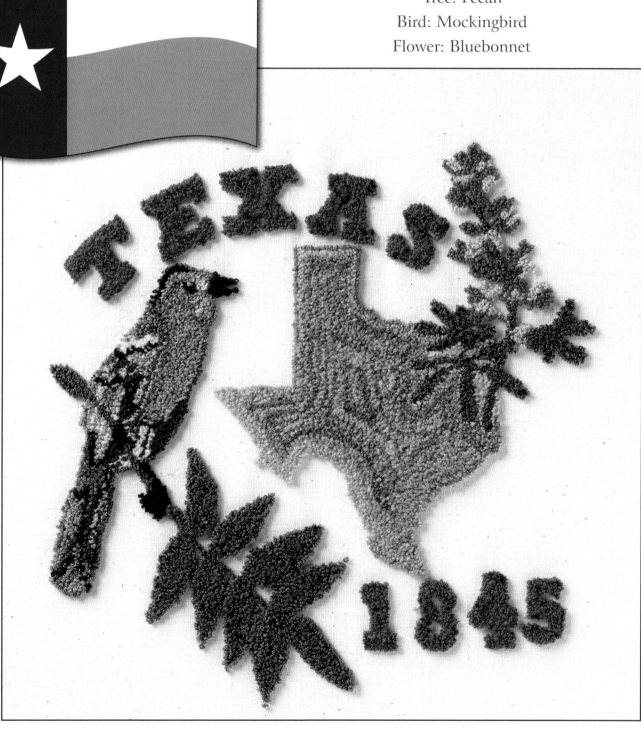

Design Element & Order to Stitch	DMC® Embroidery Floss	Notes for Stitching
1. Date	3777 Terra Cotta, dark	Stitch the date just inside the pattern lines and fill.
2. State Name	3777 Terra Cotta, dark	Stitch the state name just inside the pattern lines and fill.
3. Bluebonnets	319 Pistachio Green, dark (veins, stems, leaves) 517 Wedgewood, dark (petals) 168 Pewter, light (petals)	Stitch veins and stem. Outline and fill leaves. Stitch dark areas of petals, and then stitch light areas (refer to photo for color placement).
4. State Silhouette	111 Mustard, variegated **(2 skeins)**	Outline state and fill. Take care as you stitch around the leaves, which overlap the state outline, so you do not snag those threads.
5. Pecan Tree (branch)	433 Brown, medium (branch/bud) 319 Pistachio Green, dark (bud, stem, veins) 730 Olive Green, dark (leaves)	Stitch branch and bud. Stitch leaf veins and stem. Outline and fill in each leaf.
6. Mockingbird	310 Black (head, eye, beak, tail/wing feathers) 647 Beaver Gray, medium (breast, wing feathers) 53 Steel Gray, variegated (head, wing, tail) White (tail/wing feathers)	Stitch beak, eye and shadow on head in black. Stitch head and breast. Refer to photo and stitch wings and tail using white, black, and both grays.

UTAH

Entered Union: January 4, 1896
Beehive State
Motto: Industry
Tree: Blue Spruce
Bird: California Gull
Flower: Sego Lily

Design Element & Order to Stitch	DMC® Embroidery Floss	Notes for Stitching
1. Date	498 Red, dark	Adjust depth gauge to 5/16-inch loop length in one-strand needle to outline and fill date using one or two strands.
2. State Name	498 Red, dark	Use one-strand needle to outline and fill letters using one or two strands.
3. Blue Spruce	319 Pistachio Green, dark (light fill) 3362 Pine Green, dark (dark fill, highlight/shadow)	Stitch pistachio green areas. Fill in remaining areas with pine green, creating highlights and shadows.
4. Sego Lily (leaves/stems)	500 Blue Green, dark (outline) 3362 Pine Green, dark (fill)	Outline leaves with blue green. Fill in with pine green.
5. Sego Lily (petals)	728 Topaz (stamen/center markings) 762 Pearl Gray, light (outline) BLANC (fill)	Stitch stamen and markings in center of lily. Outline petals and fill.
6. California Gull	105 Tan/Brown, variegated (rock) 103 Royal Blue, variegated (water) 310 Black (tail, under wing, eye, beak marking) 728 Topaz (beak) BLANC (tail markings/breast) 318 Steel Gray, light (head) 413 Pewter Gray, dark (back)	Stitch outline of rock and fill in. Stitch water line. Stitch black areas of tail and under wing. Add eye and beak marking. Outline and fill beak. Add white markings on tail. Outline and fill in breast area. Outline and fill head. Outline and fill back.
7. State Silhouette	107 Carnation, variegated (**2 skeins**)	Outline and fill state shape. Take care not to catch the punched loops.

VERMONT

Entered Union: March 4, 1791
Green Mountain State
Motto: Freedom and Unity
Tree: Sugar Maple
Bird: Hermit Thrush
Flower: Red Clover

Design Element & Order to Stitch	DMC® Embroidery Floss	Notes for Stitching
1. Date	3041 Antique Violet, medium	Adjust depth gauge to 5/16-inch loop length in one-strand needle to outline and fill date using one or two strands.
2. State Name	3041 Antique Violet, medium	Use one-strand needle to outline and fill letters using one or two strands.
3. Sugar Maple	934 Black Avocado Green (trunk/branches) 3363 Pine Green, medium (foliage) 319 Pistachio Green, dark (foliage)	Outline and fill in trunk and branches. Stitch foliage using two greens, creating shadows and highlights (see photo for color placement.)
4. Red Clover (leaves/stems)	319 Pistachio Green, dark (outside leaves) 3363 Pine Green, medium (stems/inside leaves)	Stitch leaves and stems using darker green toward outside (see photo for color placement.)
5. Red Clover (petals)	315 Antique Mauve, dark (fill) 316 Antique Mauve, medium (fill) 917 Plum, medium (fill)	Stitch petals of clover using the mauve and plum colors, starting with darkest at the bottom of each petal and progressing to brightest at the tip.
6. Hermit Thrush	310 Black (eye, beak, wing markings) ECRU (breast, tail markings) 642 Beige Gray, dark (head, back, tail) 934 Black Avocado Green (legs, wing, tail, breast/head details)	Stitch head, back and tail. Stitch legs, wing and tail. Add details on breast and head. Stitch eye and beak. Add black markings on wing. Fill breast and add markings on neck and eye with ecru.
7. State Silhouette	327 Violet, dark **(2 skeins)**	Outline and fill state. Take care not to catch the punched loops.

VIRGINIA

Entered Union: June 25, 1788
Old Dominion
Motto: Thus Always To Tyrants
Tree: Flowering Dogwood
Bird: Cardinal
Flower: American Dogwood

Design Element & Order to Stitch	DMC® Embroidery Floss	Notes for Stitching
1. Date	734 Olive Green, light	Adjust depth gauge to 5/16-inch loop length in one-strand needle to outline and fill date using one or two strands.
2. State Name	734 Olive Green, light	Use one-strand needle to outline and fill letters using one or two strands.
3. Flowering Dogwood	938 Coffee Brown, dark (trunk/branches) 927 Gray Green, light (shadow lines) BLANC (fill)	Outline and fill in trunk and branches. Stitch shadow lines and fill in blossoming tree.
4. American Dogwood (leaves/branch)	938 Coffee Brown, dark (veins/branch) 734 Olive Green, light (leaf outline/fill) 927 Gray Green, light (leaf outline/fill)	Stitch leaf veins and branch. Outline and fill in leaves.
5. American Dogwood (petals)	927 Gray Green, light (outline) 734 Olive Green, light (centers) BLANC (fill)	Outline petals. Add centers of blossoms. Fill in petals.
6. Cardinal	321 Red (breast) 349 Coral, dark (back, wing, head) 310 Black (head/body markings) 111 Mustard, variegated (eye, beak, legs)	Stitch outline of breast and fill. Stitch back, wing and headl. Add markings on head and body. Stitch eye, beak and legs.
7. State Silhouette	730 Olive Green, dark (2 skeins)	Outline and fill state shape. Take care not to catch the punched loops.

WASHINGTON

Entered Union: November 11, 1889
Evergreen State
Motto: By and By
Tree: Western Hemlock
Bird: Willow Goldfinch
Flower: Coast Rhododendron

Design Element & Order to Stitch	DMC® Embroidery Floss	Notes for Stitching
1. Date	803 Baby Blue, dark	Adjust depth gauge to 5/16-inch loop length in one-strand needle to outline and fill date using one or two strands.
2. State Name	803 Baby Blue, dark	Use one-strand needle to outline and fill letters using one or two strands.
3. Western Hemlock	3031 Mocha Brown, dark (trunk/branches) 500 Blue Green, dark (pine bough bottoms) 3347 Yellow Green, medium (pine bough tops/highlights)	Stitch trunk and branches. Stitch pine boughs using darker green along bottom of branches and lighter green along tops and for highlights.
4. Coast Rhododendron (leaves/stems)	500 Blue Green, dark (veins) 3347 Yellow Green, medium (leaves)	Outline stitch leaf veins. Outline and fill leaves.
5. Coast Rhododendron (petals)	48 Baby Pink, variegated (outline) 111 Mustard, variegated (centers) ECRU (fill)	Stitch outline of each petal. Add centers. Fill petals.
6. Goldfinch	111 Mustard, variegated (neck/back/breast outline, beak, feet) 310 Black (outline, head/wing/tail markings) ECRU (wing markings) 3821 Straw (back, breast fill)	Stitch outline along neck, back and breast. Outline head, tail and wing in black. Stitch black areas of head, wing and tail. Add markings in ecru. Add beak and feet. Fill back and breast.
. State Silhouette	169 Pewter, light (**2 skeins**)	Outline and fill state. Take care not to catch the punched loops.

WEST VIRGINIA

Entered Union: June 20, 1863
Mountain State
Motto: Mountaineers Are Always Free
Tree: Sugar Maple
Bird: Cardinal
Flower: Rhododendron

Design Element & Order to Stitch	DMC® Embroidery Floss	Notes for Stitching
1. Date	301 Mahogany, medium	Adjust depth gauge to 5/16-inch loop length in one-strand needle to outline and fill date using one or two strands.
2. State Name	301 Mahogany, medium	Use one-strand needle to outline and fill letters using one or two strands.
3. Sugar Maple	869 Hazelnut Brown, dark (trunk/branches) 3346 Hunter Green (foliage shadow) 987 Forest Green, dark (foliage highlights)	Stitch trunk and branches. Stitch and fill areas of shadowed foliage . Stitch and fill areas of highlighted foliage.
4. Rhododendron (leaves/stem)	935 Avocado Green, dark (outline/veins) 987 Forest Green, dark (fill)	Outline leaves and stitch veins. Fill leaves.
5. Rhododendron (petals)	107 Carnation, variegated (outline) 48 Baby Pink, variegated (fill) 111 Mustard, variegated (centers)	Stitch outlines of petals. Add centers. Fill petals.
6. Cardinal	666 Bright Red (body fill) 347 Salmon, dark (wing fill) 310 Black 301 Mahogany, medium (beak/legs) 111 Mustard, variegated (eye)	Stitch black areas first (refer to photo). Add beak and legs. Add eye. Fill in wing area. Outline and fill in remaining areas.
7. State Silhouette	111 Mustard, variegated (**2 skeins**)	Outline and fill state. Take care not to catch the punched loops.

WISCONSIN

Entered Union: May 29, 1848
Badger State
Motto: Forward
Tree: Sugar Maple
Bird: Robin
Flower: Wood Violet

Design Element & Order to Stitch	DMC® Embroidery Floss	Notes for Stitching
1. Date	157 Cornflower Blue, light	Adjust depth gauge to 5/16-inch loop length in one-strand needle to outline and fill date using one or two strands.
2. State Name	157 Cornflower Blue, light	Use one-strand needle to outline and fill letters using one or two strands.
3. Sugar Maple	921 Copper (leaf outline/veins) 301 Mahogany, medium (leaves) 3064 Desert Sand (leaves) 947 Burnt Orange (leaves)	Outline leaves and stitch veins. Stitch light and dark areas of leaves with corresponding shades of mahogony, desert sand and burnt orange (see photo).
4. Wood Violet (leaves/stems)	500 Blue Green, dark (stems/leaf lines) 3364 Pine Green (leaf fill)	Stitch stems and lines of leaves. Fill leaves.
5. Wood Violet (petals)	733 Olive Green, medium (centers) 823 Navy Blue, dark (around centers) 793 Cornflower Blue, medium (outline/fill)	Stitch centers. Stitch dark blue around centers. Outline and fill remaining petal areas.
6. Robin	310 Black (head, legs, feet, wing/tail markings) 3031 Mocha Brown, dark (back/wing fill) ECRU (head markings) 3820 Straw, dark (eye/beak) 947 Burnt Orange (breast)	Stitch eye and beak. Outline and fill head. Stitch head markings. Add legs and feet. Stitch markings on wing and tail. Fill remaining back and wing areas. Outline and fill breast.
7. State Silhouette	161 Gray Blue (**2 skeins**)	Outline and fill state. Take care not to catch the punched loops.

WYOMING

Entered Union: July 10, 1890
Equality State
Motto: Equal rights
Tree: Cottonwood
Bird: Western Meadowlark
Flower: Indian Paintbrush

Design Element & Order to Stitch	DMC® Embroidery Floss	Notes for Stitching
1. Date	830 Golden Olive, dark	Adjust depth gauge to 5/16-inch loop length in one-strand needle to outline and fill date using one or two strands.
2. State Name	830 Golden Olive, dark	Use one-strand needle to outline and fill letters using one or two strands.
3. Cottonwood	801 Coffee Brown, dark (trunk/branches) 934 Black Avocado Green (foliage) 3362 Pine Green, dark (foliage)	Outline and fill trunk and branches. Using one strand darker green and two strands lighter green in needle, stitch areas of foliage.
4. Indian Paintbrush (leaves/stems)	3362 Pine Green, dark	Stitch stems. Outline and fill in leaves.
5. Indian Paintbrush (petals)	350 Coral, medium (large flowers) 817 Coral Red, dark (small flowers/buds)	Stitch larger flowers. Stitch smaller flowers and buds.
6. Western Meadowlark	310 Black (markings/eye) 801 Coffee Brown, dark (markings/beak) B5200 Snow White (back fill, head) 356 Terra Cotta, medium (legs/feet) 445 Lemon, light (breast) 105 Tan Brown, variegated (rock)	Adjust depth gauge to 5/16-inch loop length in one-strand needle to work the bird. Stitch black and brown markings on bird, including beak and eye. Fill in areas of white. Outline and fill breast. Add legs and feet. Outline and fill rock.
7. State Silhouette	3852 Straw, dark **(2 skeins)**	Outline and fill state. Take care not to catch the punched loops. If date becomes buried, stitch a couple of rows around numbers with a lower loop height. Fill remaining state shape with a longer loop.

PROJECT GALLERY

Pillows

To embellish a purchased pillow with your punch needle project, begin by trimming the weaver's cloth to approximately 1" around your design. Turn and press edges of the weaver's cloth under 1/4". Center and pin design to pillow top and secure with a blanket stitch.

To decorate with a ribbon trim, follow the instructions above but secure weaver's cloth to pillow with a basting stitch. Frame the design with ribbon using a blind stitch to secure it in place.

Scrapbook

Create a customized scrapbook cover by trimming the weaver's cloth 1" around your design. Cut a frame out of scrapbook paper to fit the state design. Using fabric or craft glue, glue around the outside edges of the weaver's cloth and the paper frame. Layer the pieces on the scrapbook cover.

Bag

Decorate a purchased tote bag with your punch needle design by trimming the weaver's cloth approximately 1-1/2" around the design. Center your state design on the tote and sew a decorative stitch 1/2" to 3/4" around the punch needle. Create the fringe by removing the loose threads of the weaver's cloth. Trim fringe to desired length.

Frame

To frame your punch needle design, press the weaver's cloth around the design. Trim, leaving 2" around outside. Cut a piece of 1/4" thick foam core to fit your frame. Center the design on the foam core and secure to sides with 1/2" sequin pins. Place the finished punch needle into a photo matte and frame.

112